Entertainment WEEKLY

1998 YEARBOOK

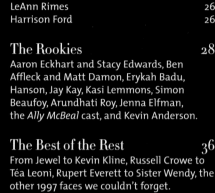

1998 YEAR BOOK

EDITOR
Alison Gwinn

SENIOR EDITOR
Nancy Bilyeau

ART DIRECTOR
Timothy Jones

PICTURE EDITOR
Sarah Rozen

ASSOCIATE EDITORS
Matthew McCann Fenton, Wook Kim, Alice King, Jill Laurinaitis

DESIGN ASSOCIATE
Catherine Mann

ASSOCIATE PICTURE EDITOR
Michael Kochman

ASSISTANT PICTURE EDITORS
Deborah Dragon, Donna Lacey, Janene Outlaw

REPORTERS
Carmela Ciuraru, Jason Cochran, Jessica J. Cohen, Sandy Hsieh, Kristi Huelsing, Beth Johnson, Leslie Marable, Matthew Morse, Tim Purtell, Erin Richter, Ann Sample, Louis Vogel

EDITORIAL PRODUCTION Eileen O'Sullivan, Lisa DiSapio Motti, George Sumerak

COPY CHIEF Steven Pearl

COPY EDITORS Alexandria Dionne, David Penick

EDITORIAL ASSISTANT Jay Ehrlich

ENTERTAINMENT WEEKLY CONSUMER MARKETING

CONSUMER MARKETING DIRECTOR
Monica Ray

TIME INC. HOME ENTERTAINMENT

MANAGING DIRECTOR David Gitow

DIRECTOR, CONTINUITIES AND SINGLE SALES David Arfine

DIRECTOR, CONTINUITIES AND RETENTION Michael Barrett

DIRECTOR, NEW PRODUCTS Alicia Longobardo

GROUP PRODUCT MANAGERS Robert Fox, Michael Holahan

PRODUCT MANAGERS Christopher Berzolla, Stacy Hirschberg, Amy Jacobsson, Jennifer McLyman, Dan Melore

MANAGER, RETAIL AND NEW MARKETS Thomas Mifsud

ASSOCIATE PRODUCT MANAGERS Louisa Bartle, Alison Ehrmann, Carlos Jimenez, Nancy London, Dawn Perry, Daria Raehse

ASSISTANT PRODUCT MANAGERS Meredith Shelley, Betty Su

EDITORIAL OPERATIONS DIRECTOR John Calvano

FULFILLMENT DIRECTOR Michelle Gudema

FINANCIAL DIRECTOR Tricia Griffin

ASSOCIATE FINANCIAL MANAGER Amy Maselli

MARKETING ASSISTANT Sarah Holmes

CONSUMER MARKETING DIVISION

PRODUCTION DIRECTOR John E. Tighe

BOOK PRODUCTION MANAGER Jessica McGrath

BOOK PRODUCTION COORDINATOR Joseph Napolitano

SPECIAL THANKS TO Donna Miano-Ferrara, Anna Yelenskaya

EDITOR IN CHIEF: Norman Pearlstine
EDITORIAL DIRECTOR: Henry Muller
EDITOR OF NEW MEDIA: Daniel Okrent

CHAIRMAN, CEO: Don Logan
EXECUTIVE VICE PRESIDENTS: Elizabeth Valk Long, Jim Nelson, Joseph A. Ripp

Entertainment WEEKLY

MANAGING EDITOR: James W. Seymore Jr.
EXECUTIVE EDITOR: Richard Sanders
ASSISTANT MANAGING EDITORS: Peter Bonventre, Jeannie Park
GENERAL EDITOR: David Hajdu
DESIGN DIRECTOR: John Korpics
PHOTOGRAPHY DIRECTOR: Mary Dunn
L.A. BUREAU CHIEF: Cable Neuhaus
ART DIRECTOR: Geraldine Hessler
PICTURE EDITOR: Doris Brautigan
SENIOR EDITORS: George Blooston, Doug Brod, Mark Harris, Albert Kim, John McAlley, Maggie Murphy, Mary Kaye Schilling
SPECIAL PROJECTS EDITOR: Alison Gwinn
DIRECTOR OF RESEARCH SERVICES: Annabel Bentley
MANAGING ART DIRECTOR: Joe Kimberling
EDITORIAL MANAGER: Lauren Kunkler
STAFF EDITORS: Jamie Bufalino, Jess Cagle, Cynthia Grisolia, Tina Jordan
CRITIC-AT-LARGE: Ken Tucker
CRITICS: David Browne, Ty Burr, Bruce Fretts, Owen Gleiberman, Lisa Schwarzbaum
WRITERS-AT-LARGE: Dana Kennedy, Benjamin Svetkey
SENIOR WRITERS: Rebecca Ascher-Walsh, Steve Daly, Joe Flint, Jeff Gordinier, David Hochman, A.J. Jacobs, Gregg Kilday, Chris Willman
SENIOR ASSOCIATE EDITOR: Caren Weiner
ASSOCIATE EDITORS: Marc Bernardin, Eileen Clarke, Marion Hart, Dulcy Israel, Joe Neumaier, William Stevenson, Mitchell Vinicor, Louis Vogel, Tracy A. Walsh
STAFF WRITERS: Andrew Essex, Mike Flaherty, Kate Meyers, Christopher Nashawaty, Degen Pener, Tom Sinclair, Dan Snierson
CORRESPONDENTS: Kristen Baldwin, Suna Chang, Dave Karger
SENIOR BROADCAST CORRESPONDENT: Lisa Karlin

DESIGN
ASSOCIATE ART DIRECTOR: John Walker
ASSISTANT ART DIRECTOR: Bobby B. Lawhorn Jr.
SENIOR DESIGNER: Keith Campbell
DESIGNER: George McCalman
DESIGN ASSISTANT: Erin Whelan

PICTURES
PICTURE EDITOR, SPECIAL PROJECTS: Sarah Rozen
ASSOCIATE PICTURE EDITOR: Alice H. Babcock
ASSISTANT PICTURE EDITORS: Helena V. Ashton, Michael Kochman (L.A.), Richard B. Maltz, Michele Romero
PICTURE COORDINATOR: Luciana Chang
ASSISTANT: L. Michelle Dougherty

RESEARCH SERVICES
REPORTERS: Tim Purtell (Deputy), Jason Cochran, Shirliey Y. Fung, Kristi Huelsing, Beth Johnson, Erin Richter, Daneet Steffens
INFORMATION CENTER MANAGER: Rachel Sapienza
DEPUTY: Stacie Fenster ASSOCIATE: Sean O'Heir
ASSISTANT: Alexandria Carrion

COPY
COPY CHIEF: Ben Spier DEPUTY COPY CHIEF: Steven Pearl
COPY EDITOR: Alexandria Dionne

EW ONLINE
EDITOR: Michael Small
ART DIRECTOR: Paul Schrynemakers DEPUTY EDITOR: Mark Bautz
PRODUCTION DESIGNER: Jeff Kolber ASSOCIATE EDITOR: Stanley Olson
CORRESPONDENT: Josh Wolk TECH EVENTS PRODUCER: Chris Sizemore
EDITORIAL COORDINATOR: Gary Eng Walk
ASSISTANT PICTURE EDITOR: Rayna Evans
EDITORIAL ASSISTANT: Melinda Spaulding

PRODUCTION
MAKEUP MANAGER: Robin Kaplan
PLANT OPERATIONS MANAGER: Karen S. Doyle
PRODUCTION MANAGER: Sue Barnett
STAFF: Ray Battaglino, George L. Beke, Paul Bodley Jr., Kevin Christian, Evan J. Dong, John Goodman, Don Gordon, Robert D. Kennedy, Bill Lazzarotti, Lisa DiSapio Motti, Ann Griffith O'Connor, Lauren Planit, Eve A. Rabinovits, Tom Roemlein, Leona Smith, George Sumerak, Daniel C. Thompson

TECHNOLOGY
MANAGER: James S. Mittelmark
SENIOR TECHNOLOGY COORDINATORS: Jeffrey Cherins, Godwin Mensah
TECHNOLOGY COORDINATOR: Joe Russell

EDITORIAL ASSISTANTS
Rob Brunner, Kipp Erante Cheng, Daniel Fierman, Allison Gaines, Anna Holmes, Alexandra Jacobs, Tricia Laine, Shawna Malcom, Troy Patterson

ADMINISTRATION
ASSISTANT TO THE MANAGING EDITOR: Rita Silverstein
STAFF: Carole Willcocks

CONTRIBUTORS
Judith I. Brennan, Pat H. Broeske, Vanessa V. Friedman, L.S. Klepp, Gene Lyons, Lois Alter Mark, Margot Mifflin, Jim Mullen, Alanna Nash, Lawrence O'Toole, David Poland, Ira Robbins, Michael Sauter, Stephen Schaefer, Heidi Siegmund Cuda, Bob Strauss

PRESIDENT: Michael J. Klingensmith
PUBLISHER: Michael J. Kelly
CONSUMER MARKETING DIRECTOR: Monica Ray
DIRECTOR OF FINANCE & ADMINISTRATION: George H. Vollmuth
ASSOCIATE PUBLISHER: David S. Morris
PRODUCTION DIRECTOR: Carol A. Mazzarella
ASSOCIATE PUBLISHER: Daniel J. Osheyack
DIRECTOR OF PROMOTION AND PUBLIC AFFAIRS: Sandy W. Drayton

TIME INC.
SENIOR EXECUTIVE EDITOR: Frank Lalli
EXECUTIVE EDITORS: Joëlle Attinger, José M. Ferrer III
DEVELOPMENT EDITOR: Jacob Young
TIME INC. EDITORIAL SERVICES: Sheldon Czapnik (Director); Claude Boral (General Manager); Thomas E. Hubbard (Photo Lab); Lany Walden McDonald (Research Center); Beth Bencini Zarcone (Picture Collection); Thomas Smith (Technology); James Macove (Marketing);
TIME INC. EDITORIAL TECHNOLOGY
Paul Zazzera (Vice President); Damien Creavin (Director)

HOT Sheet

{ *What the country was talking about in 1997* }

1 BRAD AND GWYNETH No one saw *Seven Years in Tibet*. They'd all just seen *Two Years in the Tabloids*.

2 HANSON The year's surprise hit. The record company took a chance and hired a band with no prior convictions.

3 *ER* LIVE They're already working on next season's ratings stunt. George Clooney will save a man who's injured while zipping up a batsuit.

4 TIGER WOODS The highest-paid golfer in the world. If you don't count Michael Jordan.

5 *STAR WARS* A 20-year-old film *can* get people to leave the house. But anyone with home movies could tell you that.

6 SEPTUPLETS The lead story for weeks on *The Itty-Bitty, Itsy-Bitsy Nighty-Night News With Tom Brokaw.*

7 *MEN IN BLACK* Will Smith and Tommy Lee Jones save the entire planet. And most of the jobs at Sony.

8 BEANIE BABIES The collectible toys taught kids life lessons. Like how to be greedy, calculating, and possessive.

9 LANDING ON MARS If we can put a rover on the red planet, why can't we get satellite shots of nude celebrities?

10 *SEINFELD* SALARIES The cast asked for a million an episode. Or what Bill Gates made while you read that.

11 CLONING We're a step away from cloning humans. China can stop worrying about not having enough people.

12 HEAVEN'S GATE The cult who left their "containers" to join Hale-Bopp. Too bad they were no deposit, no return.

13 MARILYN MANSON Some cities wanted to ban him for promoting Satan worship. How provincial can you get?

14 VIRTUAL PETS Why pay $15 for something that needs constant attention when you can get a husband for free?

15 FRANK GIFFORD He was tricked into a hotel rendezvous. They told him he was going to meet Marv Albert.

ILLUSTRATIONS BY TOM BACHTELL

APPLAUSE

ILLUSTRATION BY GENE GRIEF

The Entertainers

IT WAS A YEAR OF SAFETY AND RISK, reassurance and provocation. We applauded the courage of Ellen DeGeneres for using her sitcom as a platform for challenging sexual stereotypes, yet we also cheered on those conventionally cutie-pie pop tarts, the Spice Girls. At the same time that we thrilled to the brash sting of Chris Rock's comedic genius, we enjoyed the goin'–down–as–smooth–as–Cherry Coke country hits of LeAnn Rimes. Sigourney Weaver, in her portrayal of a sexually overheated yet emotionally frozen '70s housewife in *The Ice Storm*, dared us to dislike her, while another A-list performer, Harrison Ford, dared us to like him even more, as a punch-throwing, high-flying American president in *Air Force One*. But it was probably director James Cameron, with his film *Titanic*, who best captured the contradictory tone of 1997: After months of delay—and relentless sniping from the press—the director ended the year a critics' darling, all in the service of a movie that, despite its dazzling special effects and grandiose packaging, was essentially a simple, old-fashioned Hollywood love story. As with the other creative efforts we salute in the following pages, it was a voyage well worth making.

{*the* Entertainers}

By coming out on TV (and in life), this comic re-liever made showbiz history—and proved that in terms of creativity, honesty *is* the best policy

CELEBRITIES THINKING ABOUT DECLARING THEIR SEXUAL ORIENTATION AS A means of snagging EW's Entertainer of the Year award, take note: Ellen DeGeneres does not win the 1997 prize just because her announcement was the most highly advertised acknowledgment of homosexuality since Walt Whitman burbled, "I celebrate myself, and sing myself."

She's not No. 1 simply because, in allowing her alter ego, Ellen Morgan, to discover her sexuality on *Ellen* in the show's fourth season, the star made history by staging the first coming out of a lead character on a network sitcom. Or because, in doing so, *Ellen* has become a better sitcom, one that finally showcases the comedian to best advantage. Or because the star and her 28-year-old girlfriend, actress Anne Heche, have become the most photographed, most demonstrative lesbian lovebirds in paparazzi history.

In the end, Ellen DeGeneres is Entertainer of the Year because, at a time when acceptance is the word of the day but by no means entirely the deed, and when more and more of the sizable population of homosexual men and women working in the entertainment industry today are weighing the risks of coming out themselves, DeGeneres, 39, allowed herself to become a poster girl—for honesty. She risked her professional reputation for personal freedom. She did good, important, entertaining work, work that continues to shape the public discourse. And she found love. Not bad for a year's accomplishments.

"All I wanted to do was a very good show and at the same time free myself," Ellen swears, with the kind of plainspokenness that characterizes her comedy style. (Now's the moment to credit ABC, which continues to take heat from skittish advertisers, anxious affiliates, and angry conservatives; now's also the time to note that *Ellen* is running an upper-middle-of-the-pack 33rd for the season and consistently winning its 9:30 p.m. Wednesday time slot.)

Of course, that doesn't mean pigeonholing herself as That Lesbian Girl. In the upcoming dark comedy *Goodbye Lover*, DeGeneres plays it straight as a cop; next she'll costar with Matthew McConaughey as a straight cable executive in *Ed TV*. At the same time, keeping *Ellen* honest matters deeply. "ABC probably thought, 'Well, she'll just be gay, but she'll still get her foot caught in the blind and spill water, and we'll never mention this ever again,'" she wagers. "But if somebody discovers at 35 years old they're gay, there's a transition period. I wanted to get into a relationship [with Lisa Darr as Ellen Morgan's girlfriend] because I wanted to show that this is a wonderful thing."

It's too soon to tell what the long-term cultural effect will be of the sexual awakening of Ellen Morgan—or, indeed, how long a life *Ellen* has in store. (ABC will decide in May whether to keep the sitcom going; Lifetime will run it in syndication.) But it's not too soon to honor this plucky entertainer for proving the value of that old piece of advice offered by high school English teachers everywhere: Write what you know. —*Lisa Schwarzbaum*

With twin Emmys, a book, a comedy album, and
a fistful of film roles, he's a rock for all ages

THIS ISN'T THE FIRST TIME CHRIS ROCK'S BEEN ONE OF EW'S ENTER-
tainers of the Year. Five years ago, he was chosen as part of the
cast of the resurgent *Saturday Night Live*. He's experienced some
lean times since then, most notably playing second banana to
fellow *SNL* vet Chris Farley in *Beverly Hills Ninja*. "I worked on that
movie for four days, and they put out ads like it was *The Defiant
Ones*," carps Rock, slipping off his Nikes (he's the voice of company puppet Li'l Penny) and kicking back in his Manhattan office.

"Don't call it a comeback/'Cause I been here for years," Rock
raps à la LL Cool J. Still, he hasn't had many years like '97: He won
two Emmys for his HBO special *Bring the Pain* and two CableACEs
for his self-titled HBO talk show. He also wrote the well-reviewed
humor book *Rock This!* and released *Roll With the New*, an album
that spawned the heavily played video "Champagne."

"*It was a verrrry good year/When I was 31*," croons Rock, 32, im-
personating another idol, Frank Sinatra. "*I hosted the MTV Video
Awards/And it was funnnn*." ("The Spice Girls sold 10 million
records?" he asked the crowd, including the pop quintet, in one
monologue. "How come I don't know anyone who bought one?")

"Chris has always been smarter than the average comedian,
but his material wasn't always smarter," says *The Chris Rock Show*
consulting producer Nelson George, who wrote the rap mockumentary *CB4* with Rock in 1993. "He used to do [female geni-
talia] jokes. Now he does *relationship* jokes."

He's also unafraid to turn his wit on politics. (Rock on Jesse
Jackson: "He started rhyming just a little too much. Just got silly.")
"I'm a Democrat with a Republican wallet," Rock says. "I'm going
to give almost 50 percent of my money to the government this
year, and I'm not a doctor or a lawyer. I have an occupation where
I'm hot, then I'm cold. I may never make this money again."

Still, Rock isn't cooling off any time soon: He'll provide the voice
of a guinea pig in the Eddie Murphy remake of *Dr. Dolittle*, play
the apostle Rufus in Kevin Smith's *Dogma*, and costar as a cop in
Lethal Weapon 4. One month before *LW4* is set to start shooting,
Rock hadn't seen a script yet, "but this movie isn't falling on me.
The only thing I can do wrong is not be funny."

Not much danger of that. But does Rock risk exhaustion with
his multimedia assault? "Chris is tired," says George. "This has
been a hell of a year, and he's a skinny guy." As for Rock, he just
wants to express himself: "I've got ideas in my head, things I
want to do. I've got jokes to tell." Rock on. —*Bruce Fretts*

PHOTOGRAPH BY ANDREW BRUSSO

Fifteen minutes of fame? Try a year. In 1997, five Brit-chick pop rockers took the world by storm. So what's next?

SCARY, BABY, GINGER, SPORTY, AND...WHAT'S THE LAST ONE AGAIN? SALTY? Snoozy? Already the memory dims. And that, when you think about it, is the amazing thing about the Spice Girls. They started 1997 as the hottest girl group on the planet—ultimately selling more than 19 million albums—and seemed to end it as a bit of trivia for the Game Show Network. In just 12 months, these five Brit lasses took in the entire swirling circle of fame—the hit song and movie deal, the magazine covers and money fights, the backlash and breakup rumors—all in less time than it takes most groups to trash their first hotel room.

It was a riveting spectacle, even for those with *good* musical taste. Overnight, they were *everywhere*—on the radio with their hit "Wannabe," in bookstores with their fast-selling *Girl Power!*, even peddling their own brand of junk food (in England, fans munched on Spice potato crisps and Spice candy bars). Blink and you might have missed them at the Cannes film festival, performing on the Croisette. Or in South Africa, where Nelson Mandela reportedly said that meeting them was "one of the greatest moments of my life." Or being photographed with Prince Harry.

But then the cruel cycle of celebrityhood turned inexorably against them. There was that messy business with their manager, Simon Fuller, fired last November as rumors spread of an affair with Baby Spice. There was Barcelona, where they were booed at an awards show. Their second album, *Spiceworld*, sold only 100,000 copies in the U.S. its first two weeks; their movie of the same name got panned by European critics; even their chocolate bar got in trouble for violating European cocoa-content standards. That's right, even as *candy* the Spice Girls were having trouble cutting it.

The meltdown was as spectacular as the rise, and in some ways just as synthetic. A totally artificial creation (none of the Spices were real musicians), constructed of equal parts hype and marketing, they were designed *not* to last—disposable entertainment at its finest. By year's end, their fall seemed inevitable. Of course, it's possible the Spice Girls still have one or two seconds ticking in their 15 minutes. In which case, expect one last glorious gasp from the Prefab Five: The Spice Comeback. —*Benjamin Svetkey*

The

Girls

Don't hate them because they're beautiful—this is one screwed-up family. (And isn't it great to feel their pain?)

SOMETIMES, THE CRUMMIEST LUCK MAKES THE YUMMIEST TV. TAKE, FOR EXAMPLE, THE Fox drama *Party of Five*. With the number of Kleenex crises these cursed orphans have faced over the last three and a half years, they could write the *A-to-Z Dictionary of Life's Bummers* (Abortion, Betrayal, Cancer, Death, Estrangement...).

That said, every Wednesday night we watch—in ever greater numbers. Or rather, we hover on the edge of our sofas, throwing hands up in frustration one moment, wiping eyes the next. We join this *Party* because no matter which gorgeous-looking Salinger is in peril—Charlie (Matthew Fox), moody-as-all-hell father figure; Bailey (Scott Wolf), clue-starved alcoholic living with sweet, sensible ex-girlfriend Sarah (Jennifer Love Hewitt); Julia (Neve Campbell), quasi-mature teen struggling with jelly-brained husband Griffin (Jeremy London); Claudia (Lacey Chabert), over-attuned ninth grader stuck watching little Owen—it's not about some tragedy du jour. It's about downright gooey things like *family* and *love*. It's about flawed folks who confront mundane problems and deconstruct them in note-perfect, "That's *so* not the point" twentysomething-speak.

In 1997, *Party*—the thinking person's soap, if not prime time's classiest drama—crashed into pop consciousness, attracting millions of new devotees. And the Little Drama That Could offered some of TV's most gripping recent story lines: Bailey's battle with alcoholism last spring showcased Wolf as a tightly wound emotional spring box who exploded in a brutal intervention. The tension shifted in the fall to Charlie's painfully detailed struggle with Hodgkin's disease. Meanwhile, the understated Campbell broke out on the big *Scream*; Love Hewitt scored in *I Know What You Did Last Summer* (look for her in the teen comedy *The Party* and a *Summer* sequel in '98); and Chabert is costarring in the upcoming *Lost in Space*. So what's their magic appeal? They aren't slacking their way to success. In fact, they care *a lot*. "I don't think you *can* care too much," Wolf says earnestly. "I remember calling [*Party* exec producer] Amy Lippman once and leaving a message that said, 'Hey, it's me, Bailey. Gimme a call.' And her husband said, 'Does he actually *like* people to call him Bailey?' I guess I take what I'm doing very seriously." And for that, we angst you very much. —*Dan Snierson*

The Cast of
Party of
Five

{the Entertainers}

The son also rises: As Dylan junior wins the hearts of teenagers, his still-raging papa shows he can still rule our minds

WHEN BOB DYLAN WAS BORN IN '41, HIS PARENTS BESTOWED UPON HIM THE name Robert Zimmerman. Years later, wise to the notion that every legend-in-the-making needs a cool handle, the troubadour from Minnesota borrowed a stage name from Welsh poet Dylan Thomas. It was Thomas, of course, who set down these famous words about death: "Do not go gentle into that good night / Old age should burn and rave at close of day / Rage, rage against the dying of the light."

Bob Dylan almost died in 1997. A condition called pericarditis caused the sac around his heart to swell, and he spent much of the early summer on his back, in agony, on meds. Then, like a cyclone that whips into a fury after nearly tapering out at sea, Dylan started raging. He grabbed the ax and went back on the road. He released his toughest batch of songs since the days before disco: *Time Out of Mind*, an album about death—a fierce, swampy, blues-haunted lesson in how to burn into old age. Dylan—yep, the "Don't follow leaders" guy, the "With God on Our Side" guy—even posed with the President and played for the Pope. While one-hit wonders rained down on radio like a plague of locusts ("The top stars of today, you won't even know their names two years from now," Dylan forewarned *Newsweek*. "Five years from now, they'll be *obliterated*"), the Dylan legacy cast a long dark shadow across the badlands.

In the suburbs, meanwhile, a different Dylan legacy was making the rounds. Jakob Dylan, Bob's 28-year-old son—he of the Jimmy Dean slouch and the piercing cobalt eyes and the voice like rustling hay—emerged from his own years in the wilderness and traded in his father's Old Testament oratory for dashboard-thumping rock. As a result, Jakob's band, the Wallflowers, managed to accomplish two things that Dad rarely did: make the teenage girls scream and sell a hell of a lot of records. (The Wallflowers' *Bringing Down the Horse* went quadruple platinum.) Okay, maybe Jakob's "6th Avenue Heartache" doesn't have half the battery-acid spite of Bob's "Positively 4th Street," but "Heartache" sounds better at a party. For all their differences, Dylan the Elder and Dylan the Younger come to their craft with a devotion to old-school virtues sadly missing in global conglomo-pop. Both belong less to a specific year than to a time out of mind. Like the grim reaper snarling through a strip mall, the poet Robert Zimmerman took a look around at '97 and croaked out the creaky, gluey opening bars of his new album: "I'm walking through streets that are dead." Raging against the dying of the light never sounded so incandescent. —*Jeff Gordinier*

Producing hits—and making millions—for the likes of Mariah Carey was child's play. Now Sean Combs steps behind the mike himself as rap's big daddy.

NOW, *THIS* IS SHOWBIZ MUSCLE. DURING EACH OF PUFF DADDY'S SOLD-out fall concerts, the houselights came up. And Puffy, a.k.a. Sean Combs—the 26-year-old impresario who glamorized, revitalized, and just plain ruled rap last year—directed the throng to make three motions: Stand up, put their hands in the air, and sit down. Soon the entire arena was performing, of all things, the wave. "The wave is some silly s---," says Combs. "For hip-hop, there's never been no wave done."

Nor has rap seen anyone like Combs. Not content to be a producer and remixer (although everyone from Mariah Carey to Aretha Franklin clamors for his services) and not happy simply owning his own record company (although his Bad Boy Entertainment may have brought in more than $150 mil in 1997), Combs created Puff Daddy, his supersize alter ego, and released his own album, *No Way Out*. It sold 561,000 copies its first week. A more incredible statistic: Beginning in November 1996, six hit songs in a row either sung or produced by Combs held down the top spot on *Billboard*'s rap singles chart for 42 consecutive weeks. "Almost a whole year," he says.

Rappers have always sampled, but Puffy stepped up to the pop buffet and made meals of others' hits. Heard his single "Been Around the World"? Sure you have; it's composed mostly of samples from David Bowie and Lisa Stansfield. And the boost works. "I'll Be Missing You," his reworking of the Police's "Every Breath You Take" into a heartfelt tribute to the Notorious B.I.G., went No. 1 in 16 countries.

Critics may wail, but the result is more than the sum of his appropriations. "He's brought back fun party records," says Carey, who had a No. 1 hit with Puffy. "He's made hip-hop accessible to the masses." Fueled partly by his links to British '80s pop, Puff Daddy began his crossover just when rap was in danger of imploding after the slayings of Tupac Shakur and Biggie. On his current tour, multiracial crowds have been the norm. "It's a dream come true," he says. "I made my music for the urban community, but I want everybody to feel it." No wonder Fox is talking about a variety series called *Puffy's House*.

Combs, of course, has denied he helped provoke the tensions that took Tupac's and Biggie's lives. To his credit, he's turned his tour, dedicated to B.I.G.'s memory, into one big love-in. No, we're not talking expletive-filled odes to raw sex. They're there, but Puff Daddy also praises God, takes a moment to remember Tupac, and pleads for togetherness. "If I had no hits for the rest of my life and had Biggie, I'd do that in a minute," he says. "Me and him could be mailmen. I'd be ecstatic with that." —*Degen Pener*

PHOTOGRAPH BY ROBERT MAXWELL

Sean "Puffy" Combs

Whether she's fighting off homicidal aliens or hot-to-trot WASPs, this is one woman who knows when to get nasty

PERHAPS, WHEN YOU THINK OF SIGOURNEY WEAVER IN 1997, YOU PICTURE HER IN OUTER SPACE, yanking the tongue out of a slimy creature's mouth in *Alien Resurrection*. Or you picture her in bed, pulling away from slimy adulterer Kevin Kline in *The Ice Storm*. But Weaver's third fab performance of last year was the less widely seen *Snow White: A Tale of Terror*. This livid fairy-turned-horror tale, which premiered last August on Showtime and shortly after on video, is worth renting to see Our Sig portray the wickedest of stepmother witches. At one poignant point, Snow White cries out, "You have no heart!" and Weaver responds—quietly, firmly—"That's too simple."

Exactly. Nothing about the aggressive yet vulnerable, intelligent yet often heartless women Weaver has offered us over the past 12 months is simple. "That was my line," says Weaver proudly—she improvised it during filming and now says that inhabiting Snow White's chortlingly mean stepmother was "the most fun" role of her three in 1997, "even if the movie itself ended up being some investor's very large tax deduction."

As for the other characters, Weaver feels protective of *Alien*'s Ripley— "Sure, I give her all those muscles and my firm jaw, but she's really a poor duck totally abandoned in the universe, you know." And describing *Ice Storm* as "a haiku, compared with the epic of *Alien Resurrection*," she wishes more viewers had sympathy for Janey Carver, the film's brittle suburban swizzle stick. "When people who first saw the movie told [director] Ang [Lee] and me that Janey was 'such a bitch,' we looked at each other: Didn't they see how fragile and unhappy she was?"

Take all this as evidence that Weaver, 48, is a more interesting actress than ever. The severe gravity that characterized much of her early movie work hasn't softened so much as deepened, like the precisely etched lines around her mouth. Her long-standing, long-outgrown image is that of the stinging WASP, Yale-trained taskmistress, but "increasingly, my approach to performing is to be as totally abandoned, as unprepared and unintellectualized, as possible." And darned if you can't see just that: There's now a controlled recklessness in Weaver's acting—an often humorous skepticism in her on-screen gaze—that lends her alert intensity a wry, sexy glow. "I loved all these roles for the way each of them revved me up. Once I get that engine going, I can work for an eternity," she says.

Weaver may have picked up a reported $11 million paycheck for *Resurrection* but notes without a trace of rancor, "It's rare that I'm sent a big project from the major studios." While she's waiting, she'd like to teach an acting class. (Asked with mock severity for her qualifications, she replies playfully: "Well, I *do* know how to apply makeup.")

In 1998, she'll star in a film of Rafael Yglesias' deep-thought potboiler *Dr. Neruda's Cure for Evil*. And beyond that—ridiculous as it sounds—she's available for work. "Please write," she says, "that I'm looking for a job in the spring." —*Ken Tucker*

PHOTOGRAPH BY RUVEN AFANADOR

Sigourney Weaver

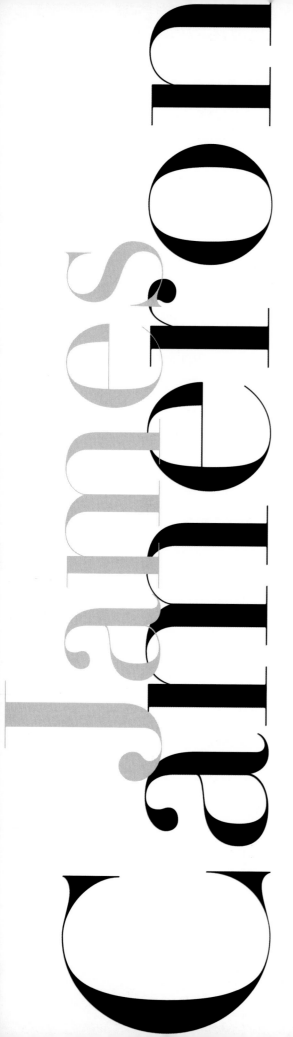

James Cameron

Like the doomed liner herself, *Titanic* once seemed headed for disaster. Now its visionary director could well be sailing into Oscar waters.

DURING THE DECADE OF RESEARCH HE DEVOTED TO THAT MOMENT ON April 14, 1912, when the *Titanic* met its fate—and especially during the two years in which he struggled to bring his magisterial, three-hour-and-17-minute, $200 million *Titanic* to the screen—James Cameron had plenty of time to contemplate what his own fate might have been if he'd booked passage on the voyage.

"Because I *do* have a sense of duty and responsibility," insists the 43-year-old writer-director-producer-editor, who endured a year of the media painting him as a reckless, megalomaniacal spendthrift, "I probably would have been one of the dumb saps who stood around on the ship. But because I am also pretty analytical, I might have had the smarts to count the number of people in the lifeboats, realize there was room for more, and swim to one to save myself without displacing anybody else." Certainly, Cameron spent most of 1997 barely escaping disaster. *Titanic* ran over schedule and over budget; it took two studios, Twentieth Century Fox and Paramount, to handle costs; it missed its initial July 2 release date. "Jim is so single-minded he refused to compromise," says Fox film chairman Bill Mechanic. "You don't set out to make one of the most expensive pictures ever made. It was a weight on his shoulders he'd have preferred not to have."

The director, whose $90 million *Terminator 2* and $120 million-plus *True Lies* weren't exactly home movies, may have been daunted by *Titanic*'s scale, but the shocking lesson the film may teach is that sometimes, bigger *is* actually better. The film won praise as a lush, richly detailed love story—one that might surprise fans of Cameron's whiz-bang adventures and muscular futuristic thrillers—and is being hailed as the front-runner for Oscar nominations.

Cameron says he connected with the *Titanic* tragedy from the first, experiencing "one of those 'click' moments. As a filmmaker who'd dealt with all these themes—the testing of a love, enormity of emotion, self-sacrifice in the face of crisis—I realized *Titanic* was a perfect backdrop for that type of storytelling." But he could never have predicted how much the film would upend his professional life, his financial life (he gave up his director's fee and profit participation as costs grew), and his personal life (after marrying *Terminator 2*'s Linda Hamilton, he deferred their honeymoon to return to editing).

Cameron has yet to decide on his next project, but if he is crowned come Oscar time, can he ever return to his old genre ways? "With *Titanic*, I give myself permission to do straight dramatic subjects," he says. "But I could go from the highest-end, big-budget science-fiction film to a very small drama and feel comfortable with either." Cameron thinking *small*? Now, *that* would be a departure. —*Gregg Kilday*

Kevin
Williamson

The horror genre was dead and buried. Now, thanks to his screamingly good scripts, it's time to be afraid—be *very* afraid.

SO WHO THE HECK IS KEVIN WILLIAMSON? IF YOU HAVE to ask, then odds are pretty good that your typical Saturday-night plans don't involve hollering at blood-splattered buxom teens to *"Get the hell out of the house!"* You see, Williamson is the guy who resurrected the played-out horror-film genre with last year's $103 million semiotic slasher sensation, *Scream*. But far from being a one-hit wonder, the 32-year-old scribe followed up *Scream* with the chiller *I Know What You Did Last Summer* and the equally (if not more) clever sequel *Scream 2*.

On paper, the secret Williamson formula seems deceptively simple: Write smart. Williamson shows teens a reflection of how they want to be seen: witty, urbane, and always armed with a perfectly barbed, sarcastic comeback. For proof, just check out his WB teen drama, *Dawson's Creek*—a fresh and hip coming-of-age TV series so realistic it makes *My So-Called Life* look like *Joanie Loves Chachi*.

Next up for Williamson is *Killing Mrs. Tingle*—a dark comedy about a group of kids and their evil schoolteacher, which he'll also direct; an as-yet-untitled self-referential sci-fi script for director Robert Rodriguez; and another in-development TV series called *Wasteland*. When all of that's done, he'll get crackin' on the script for *Scream 3*. "I feel like I've been unemployed for so long with all these stories to tell and now someone wants to hear all of them," says Williamson. "I feel like it's all going to end one day so I better take advantage of it while I can, because today's hot flavor might be gone tomorrow." Don't bet on it. —*Chris Nashawaty*

PHOTOGRAPH BY MATTHEW WELCH

Elton John

IT CAN SAFELY BE SAID THAT NO HUMAN BEING HAS EVER turned 50 quite like Elton John. Last April, he arrived at his birthday bash done up as an Über-Louis in a white wig topped with a dainty silver ship—an $80,000 outfit that included a 15-foot ostrich-feather train borne by two hunks. John did have a lot to celebrate: Soon he would embark on a world tour and release a new album, *The Big Picture*. And the stage version of *The Lion King*, for which John and Tim Rice added four songs to their original movie score, would open to record-breaking ticket sales.

Yet merely listing John's recent accomplishments is an exercise in irony. For it's not triumph that we associate with him last year, but tragedy. The image remains indelible: Sitting stone-faced at a piano in Westminster Abbey, he gave a performance of "Candle in the Wind 1997" that united us in grief. Moreover, he earmarked all his profits for the Diana, Princess of Wales, Memorial Fund.

Such good behavior could have been a bit surprising to the viewers of *Tantrums and Tiaras*, a Cinemax bio-documentary (shot by his lover) showing John to be a man short of temper, enamored of the spoils of his success, and prone to wild mood swings. Yet such are the complicated rhythms of his life and persona—and they account, at least in part, for his enduring appeal.

"I'm always going to do what I want to do," he said in *Tantrums*. By doing what he wanted in 1997, by staying true to his instincts as a performer and a man, Elton John made us appreciate him more than ever. —*Jess Cagle*

His public grieving for Princess Diana showed us that beneath the glittering diamonds and tiaras gleams pure gold

Harrison Ford

From swashbuckling space pilot to two-fisted chief executive, he gave new meaning to the saying "Built Ford Tough"

IT'S EASY TO IMAGINE HARRISON FORD IN HIS FORMER LIFE AS A CARpenter. During those lean years before *Star Wars*, *Raiders of the Lost Ark*, and the Wyoming ranch, the struggling actor paid the rent by hammering his way around Hollywood. Knowing what we know now, we picture Ford showing up in his *Witness* suspenders, wielding his power tools like a lightsaber. His craftsmanship would be solid and dependable, putting the competition to shame.

We can be sure about this because after watching Ford on screen for 25 years, we feel we know something about him. He's trustworthy. He's a man who cares about detail. And he can probably work wonders with a circular saw and a 2 by 4. In other words, we believe in Harrison Ford.

In 1997, we believed that not only could he be President but he could also single-handedly put down a terrorist takeover of Air Force One. Yes, Tom Hanks could have led our nation, but drop-kicking Kazakhstanis? Never! Ford, though, we believe.

We believe, too, that the Force is still with him. Han Solo seems as relevant today as he did two decades ago, when *Star Wars* first soared. "I was a little concerned," he says. "After all, it's 20-year-old acting."

Above all, we believe Ford is an ordinary citizen of the republic: modest, pleasantly cynical, and definitely uncomfortable with all the attention. If we were him, we could only hope we'd be a lot like him. —*DH*

PHOTOGRAPH BY NIGEL PARRY

LeAnn Rimes

IT'S AMAZING LEANN RIMES CALLS HERSELF A COUNTRY SINGER. SHE'S too young to drive a truck or to have seen combat in the Persian Gulf. She can't legally marry, so she can't really get divorced. Heck, in some cases, she's too young to take a job, let alone shove one.

Never you mind. Rimes, 15, has country down just fine. With nods to Jesus, cattle, and Patsy Cline, she turned *Blue* into the biggest debut album ever by a female country artist. The double-platinum *You Light Up My Life* topped *Billboard*'s pop and country charts, seven months after *Unchained Melody/The Early Years* debuted as the No. 1 album in America.

Sure, talent and charm alone might have catapulted Rimes from the junior-prom circuit to the Grand Ol' Big Time. But if you're looking for a more convincing answer, consider history. The last time anybody saw anything like Rimes, her name was Tanya Tucker. It was 1972; Tucker was 13; the song was "Delta Dawn." Tucker has said she didn't even understand the lyrics about a jilted woman wandering the streets, but that didn't matter. The country-crunching boomers dug it anyhow, and the song owned the charts for months.

Now the kids of those boomers—the same ones who turned Nintendo and Barney into national institutions—have picked Rimes as their favorite country cousin. So what if she can't yet drink booze or wail about her D-I-V-O-R-C-E? She'll grow into it. —*David Hochman*

At 15, she may be too young to drive, but this hard-belting country songbird is still speeding down the road to success

{the} Rookies

{Best New Movie Actors}
Aaron Eckhart
and
Stacy Edwards

IT WAS JUST A DINKY INDIE FLICK SHOT in 12 days for $25,000, but Neil LaBute's *In the Company of Men* yielded two of last year's most riveting performances. In fact, stars Aaron Eckhart, 29, and Stacy Edwards, 32, were so disturbingly true to their roles that some people still haven't forgiven them. "A lot of women are revolted when they meet me—you can see the fire in their eyes," chuckles Eckhart, who played Chad, a corporate sociopath who coolly decides to romance and brutally dump a shy deaf woman just because he can. "But I like it when people call me a prick or tell me to f--- off. It means I did a good job." Edwards, the devastated dumpee, had a similar problem: "Women would come up to me and ask me how I could *be* in such a movie," she says. Happily for both actors, others have been more receptive. Edwards has landed a gig on CBS' *Chicago Hope*, while Eckhart will costar in the cocaine-dealer drama *Thursday* and in LaBute's high-profile sophomore effort, *Your Friends and Neighbors*. "This time I'm playing the opposite of Chad," says the actor, who gained 40 pounds for the role. "A man whose wife is cheating on him." Sometimes, cinematic revenge is the sweetest kind. —*Benjamin Svetkey*

PHOTOGRAPH BY CATHERINE LEDNER

{Best New Hyphenates}
Ben Affleck
and Matt Damon

BEN AFFLECK (LEFT) AND MATT DAMON (RIGHT) WERE SUPPOSED to be rookies in '95. That's when *Good Will Hunting*, the drama they cowrote and star in as a pair of sensitive Boston toughies, would've been released by Castle Rock. But complications over who'd direct resulted in a trip to turnaround hell ("There are people I'd prefer never having met," Damon says of the experience). Two years, one distributor (Miramax), an avalanche of hype, and a dash of Oscar buzz later, the childhood friends from Cambridge, Mass., have found synchronized success as actors *and* writers. Affleck, 25, who began 1997 with great reviews as the lovesick-over-a-lesbian star of Kevin Smith's *Chasing Amy*, has wrapped this summer's thriller *Armageddon* with Bruce Willis; Damon, 27, convincingly earnest in *John Grisham's The Rainmaker*, will play the title role in Steven Spielberg's *Saving Private Ryan* (opposite Tom Hanks) and a gentlemanly killer in Anthony Minghella's *The Talented Mr. Ripley*. Damon and Affleck will also reteam as actors in Smith's religious comedy *Dogma*. No wonder the duo is awed by their *Good* fortune: Says Damon, "We're still amazed somebody bought the script."
—*Dave Karger*   PHOTOGRAPHS BY NORMAN JEAN ROY

ERYKAH BADU'S MUSIC IS A LOT LIKE THOSE gorgeous Afro-goddess headdresses she wears: towering, mysterious, coiled, and evocative of tradition. She leaves you rapt—and wrapped. There's something conservative in her sound—sultry echoes of blues, jazz, soul—but there's an audacity in the way she fuses that tradition with hip-hop sass. She's also got one hell of a voice. On last autumn's *Live* album, you can practically hear the audience break into chills as Badu's pipes navigate the serpentine grooves of "On and On." Take that song's title as an omen. The double-platinum debut of *Baduizm*—along with Badu's loving take on Curtis Mayfield's "A Child With the Blues," an Oscar-worthy lullaby on the *Eve's Bayou* soundtrack—suggests that this 26-year-old child of the blues is destined to become a matriarch in the very tradition that nurtured her. —*Jeff Gordinier*

{Best New Female Singer}
Erykah Badu

{Best New Band}
Hanson

THEY WERE **1997**'S *OTHER* BIG POP PHENOMENON THAT YOU WANTED to love to hate—only you couldn't because, it turned out, *these* kids had talent in as much abundance as pluck. Long after "Posh" and "Sporty" are consigned to the Trivial Pursuit bin—and well after the teen mags have moved on to the next big little thing—it's possible the brothers Hanson will still be crafting pleasures as indelible as "MMMBop." The youngest, Zac, at 11, can actually play the drum kit he's almost able to see over; the eldest, Isaac, 17, will eventually be able to concentrate more on songwriting than babysitting; and heartthrobby Taylor, 14, has handily survived the voice change that arrived between *Middle of Nowhere* and the Christmas album *Snowed In*. Not since the Jackson 5 has pubescence been this much fun—and doggone, they seem so well-adjusted, they won't ever have to commiserate with Liz Taylor. —*Chris Willman*   PHOTOGRAPH BY FRANK W. OCKENFELS 3

TECHNICALLY SPEAKING, JAMIROQUAI'S FOOTLOOSE FRONTMAN, 28-YEAR-OLD JAY (JASON) KAY, ISN'T EXACTLY A ROOKIE: *TRAVELLING WITHOUT Moving*, the British interstellar-funk collective's hit CD, was actually their third. But in 1997, Kay's closetful of stovepipe Seussian pimp chapeaus, arsenal of silky Electric Boogaloo dance steps, and honey-slick Stevie Wonder-esque vocal cords crossed over to the American pop mainstream. Every time you flipped on MTV, there was Kay, slip-sliding his way across a roomful of harrowing treadmills, crooning "Virtual Insanity," floating like some sort of youthful incarnation of the Godfather of Soul. But it would be a slight to reduce the wispy Manchester-bred singer-songwriter to the sum samplings of his '70s slap-bass funk forefathers. After all, in a year when electronica was supposed to revolutionize music, Kay managed to break out of the pack by realizing that the most important musical ingredient is, was, and ever shall be soul. —*Chris Nashawaty*   PHOTOGRAPH BY GREG SCAFFIDI

{Best New Male Singer}
Jay Kay of *Jamiroquai*

SINCE THEY WERE INSPIRED BY RECOLLECTIONS OF HER FAMILY, THE characters of the Southern drama *Eve's Bayou* lived with Kasi Lemmons for years before she committed them to paper. "I thought it would be a movie when I was older and wiser," says the 34-year-old actress (look closely and you'll find her in *The Silence of the Lambs* as Jodie Foster's FBI-trainee room-mate). "But it got to the point where I'd dream about them. I let the story come as a gift to myself." A gift that keeps on giving: Lemmons' independently made writing-directing debut won critical hosannas and grossed more than three times its $4 million budget. "I'm happy, I'm fulfilled, I'm full," says Lemmons, who's now adapting the 1992 suspense novel *The Impersonator*, which her husband, actor Vondie Curtis Hall (*Chicago Hope*), will direct. After that, she plans to head behind the camera again. "I don't want to give up acting," she says, "but there's a part of me that feels I have more rarefied stuff to offer as a director." We couldn't agree more. —*Rebecca Ascher-Walsh*   PHOTOGRAPH BY JO ANN TOY

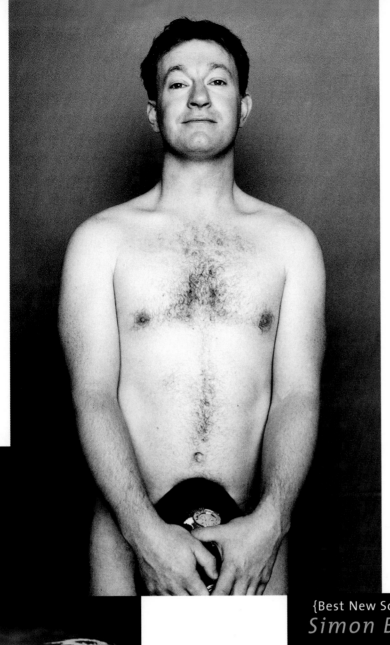

HOLLYWOOD HACKS TAKE NOTE: YOU CAN *have* your dinosaurs, your space critters, your bouncing green goo. In the end, no computerized sleight of hand is funnier, stranger, or scarier than the human body. Last year, Simon Beaufoy gave the world *The Full Monty*—an indie script about a band of pale, lumpy Englishmen who take off their clothes for money— and the world lined up to take a peek. But it wasn't Beaufoy's pelvis-pumping spectacle that made the $3 million movie a triumph (with a worldwide gross of more than $100 million). The real credit goes to the small moments in the script—those tiny scenes in which the 30-year-old British writer captured a man's ambivalent feelings about father- hood and unemployment, disco dancing and G-strings. As star Robert Carlyle puts it, "The comedy stemmed from real situations and real people." We bought tickets to see those people strip—and strip they did. Down to that most inti- mate of organs, the human heart. —*JG*
PHOTOGRAPH BY ANJA GRABERT

{Best New Screenwriter}
Simon Beaufoy

{Best New Import}
Arundhati Roy

DON'T CALL ARUNDHATI ROY A WRITER: THE 37-YEAR-OLD EX–AEROBICS INSTRUCTOR AND FORMER architecture student doesn't believe in "professions." Yet she devoted four-plus years to her glimmering, densely poetic first novel, *The God of Small Things*, in which tragedy and squalor envelop a pair of half-Hindu, half-Christian South Indian twins and their unconventional family. The work has more than 200,000 copies in print Stateside and landed Britain's prestigious Book- er Prize (among past winners: Michael Ondaatje's *The English Patient*). John Updike called it "a Tiger Woodsian debut," and Roy returns the compliment, naming him among her favorite Amer- ican authors. Other literary influences? James Joyce, D.H. Lawrence, and Vladimir Nabokov— whose scandal-tinged ranks she joined when a lawyer, outraged by *God*'s intercaste sex scenes, filed obscenity charges in her native Kerala, India. But he can't stop Roy—who says she has no interest in a movie deal—from using her $1.5 million advance to "pursue with renewed vigor my commitment to doing as little as possible." A writer? Nah. —*Alexandra Jacobs*

{Best New TV Actress}
Jenna Elfman

MAYBE SHE HAD TOO MUCH SUGAR AS A KID. MAYBE SHE RECENTLY WON A TRISTATE LOTTERY. OR MAYBE SHE'S GOT ANTS IN HER PANTS. WHAT else could explain the hepped-up bolt of fun that came shooting through prime time last fall in the form of Jenna Elfman? Don't bother asking the 26-year-old actress. "Yup," she offers, "it's the catnip." Whatever it is, America's biting. Tickled by Elfman's scrunch-nosed cuteness and loopy charm, viewers quickly glommed on to her free-spirited yoga instructor in ABC's sappy-go-lucky comedy *Dharma & Greg*, turning the show into one of last fall's only new hits. For Elfman, though, it was hardly a stretch. "I'm *totally* goofy," she says. "It's not an act. I have no limits on goofiness. To the degree that something's inappropriate, I *make* it appropriate." Right on, hippie chick. —*Dan Snierson*   PHOTOGRAPH BY KATE GARNER

ALLY MCBEAL HAS BIG DOE EYES AND WOBBLY legs ending in black, hooflike business heels; she's a dear deer with a law degree. But Calista Flockhart's fearless portrayal of a quivering corporate fawn is just one facet of the season's most engaging thespian menagerie. At home, slinky roommate-pal DA Renee (Lisa Nicole Carson) licks at spoonfuls of ice cream, shakes her thick mane of hair, and purrs reassurance. At work, Ally's boss, Richard Fish (Greg Germann), is a shyster shark with bright eyes and wit, while Peter MacNicol's John Cage sits blinking—he's a perpetually startled owl of eccentricity. Blond thorough-bred Georgia (Courtney Thorne-Smith) and stud hubby Billy (Gil Bellows) drive many of Ally's fantasies, even as Elaine (Jane Krakowski), the office's officious, wiggly whippet of a secretary, nips at everyone's heels. Where else could creator David E. Kelley's avid attorney animals thrive but on Fox? —*Ken Tucker*

PHOTOGRAPH BY DAVID JENSEN

{Best New Cast}
The Ensemble of
Ally McBeal

GROWING UP IN CATHOLIC SCHOOLS, KEVIN Anderson thought the last thing he'd ever want to portray was a priest. "I would've rather played James Bond," he admits. Now, on ABC's controversial *Nothing Sacred*, he's Ray, *Father* Ray—and each stirring week, his faith is shaken. "Spiritual growth is not set in stone," says the actor. "It's something that has to evolve." That's not an arc most actors can (or are asked to) convey, but Anderson had a premium on it in 1997: first in the film *Eye of God*, as a born-again ex-con whose zeal masks residual darkness, then on *Sacred*, where Ray's doubts and cynicism mask an inner strength. Anderson, 37, is "still a young man, but as he's matured," says exec producer Richard Kramer, "he's crossed the line into this place where there's something in his eyes that has *seen more*." We confess: We're intrigued. —*CW*

{Best New TV Actor}
Kevin Anderson

35

Best {of the} Rest

UP FROM DOWN UNDER

RUSSELL CROWE

AFTER WATCHING Russell Crowe beat up the bad guys in *L.A. Confidential*, you might hesitate to put a shrimp on this Aussie's barbie. That would be a big mistake. Crowe's complex portrayal of a tormented cop in the City of Angels was so riveting that he stole the movie from the ultimate scene-stealer himself, Kevin Spacey. Still, after 18 films, Crowe's not buying oceanfront property in California quite yet: "The saying where I come from is 'Reviews are fish-and-chip paper.' You've got to get totally used to rejection [in the film business]. I only get a job in America, it would seem, when everyone else is distracted."

PHOTOGRAPH BY DAN WINTERS

LEATHER & LACE
JEWEL

"WEIRD" IS HOW 23-year-old Jewel Kilcher describes the fame that her 5 million-selling debut album, *Pieces of You*, has brought. The Alaska native (she grew up in a cabin without electricity) started out singing with her dad in bars—and was discovered years later while performing in a California coffeehouse and sleeping in a van. Her soaring soprano has made her an MTV mainstay, with two Grammy nominations and a slew of magazine covers to her credit. It sure beats the way she used to pay bills—"bucking hay bales, ditchdigging, cow milking, waitressing." Today, the only thing Jewel's waiting on is those big fat royalty checks.

HE'S SO LOVELY

SEAN PENN

BACK FROM HIS NEAR BRUSH with retirement and fresh from living in an Airstream camper for three years (after his Malibu, Calif., home burned down), Sean Penn returned to the land of the living in 1997 with an acting trifecta: a troubled rich boy in *The Game*, a blustering gambler in *U-Turn*, and a mentally frail husband in *She's So Lovely*. Off screen, the onetime brawler and ex–Madonna mate, who wed Robin Wright in April 1996, offered these words of marital wisdom: "I don't like monotony. But if you want the same thing every day, f--- somebody new. If you want endless diversity, stay with the same one."

PHOTOGRAPH BY KURT MARKUS

YA GOTTA HAVE ART
SISTER WENDY

A *BAYWATCH* BABE she's not. So just why is Sister Wendy Beckett—who never even *watched* TV, let alone appeared on it—getting ready for her close-up? Because in 1997 this 67-year-old bucktoothed, bespectacled British nun became the PBS poster girl for fine art. Her passion for painting borders on the erotic: Standing before a masterpiece, she chatters away about "great balls of male erotic fury," "lovely, fluffy" pubic hair, or the length of Jesus' loincloth. All this from a cloistered nun who lives alone in a trailer? "God made the body. It's illogical for me to shy from it."

VAMP APPEAL

SARAH MICHELLE GELLAR

SHOP FOR GROOVY, HIGH-HEELED BOOTS. Study. Plunge stake through heart of the undead. Such is the typical to-do list for Buffy the Vampire Slayer, of the campy WB series. Credit Gellar's cheery and empathic portrayal of the kickboxing high schooler–cum–world savior for boosting Buffy to feminist heroine. (A brown belt in tae kwon do, Gellar does most of her own stunts.) The ex–soap star also appeared in two pics in 1997—*I Know What You Did Last Summer* and *Scream 2*. Something about her makes us Watchers.

BOYS IN THE ATTIC | AEROSMITH

THE YEARS OF DRUGS DIDN'T STOP THEM. Nor did the *Spiñal Tap*-esque stumbling through the early '80s, the stormy parting of the ways with their manager, or the (furiously denied) rumors of drug relapse. If Jagger and Richards are the Glitter Twins, then Aerosmith's Steven Tyler, 49 (right), and Joe Perry, 47, are the Dorian Gray Duo. Twenty-four years after the release of their debut album, *Aerosmith*, these masters of the hard-rock power ballad, the sultans of stadium swagger, are nowhere near ready to slow down. Thus the name of their 12th studio album: *Nine Lives*.

CONFIDENTIALLY YOURS

KIM BASINGER

"SHE SEDUCED ME completely," raved writer James Ellroy about Basinger's luminous portrayal of *L.A. Confidential*'s expensive call girl, a role the actress slipped into as easily as her satin peignoir. With her high-cheekboned beauty (via Cherokee ancestry) now lush, Basinger's previous incarnations as a Bond girl and a TV-movie centerfold seem light-years away. Still, K-I-M spells controversy—remember bankruptcy and Braselton, Ga.?—and '97 headlines tracked her rescue of 36 Beagle pups earmarked for medical research. With hubby Alec Baldwin mulling a run for political office, is *Basinger Shakes Up the Beltway* a future project?

PHOTOGRAPH BY ANDREW SOUTHAM/CPI

"AMERICA'S OLIVIER" dazzled: First, Kline was uproarious perfection as *In & Out*'s small-town teacher "outed" during an Academy Awards broadcast, particularly when Tom Selleck planted one on him—the year's most talked-about kiss. Then, in the shag-carpeted emotional tundra of *The Ice Storm*, he played a '70s suburbanite grappling with slippery sexual mores (as well as Sigourney Weaver). That rare critic's darling who's also a crowd-pleaser, Kline plumbed the elusive terrain of the heart to reveal each character's humanity. Then he capped it all by performing *Ivanov* on Broadway. Royal good show!

NIC'S KNACK
NICOLAS CAGE

LITTLE DID WE KNOW back when Nicolas Cage was munching a cockroach in *Vampire's Kiss* and swiping babies in *Raising Arizona* that what he *really* wanted to be was...an action hero. It was Cage's year of living dangerously. Whether battling a planeful of inmates in *Con Air* or a two-faced John Travolta in *Face/Off,* he took his duties seriously: "I ate salt-free tuna, fat-free pretzels, ran five to six miles a day. I wanted to look ripped but not bulky." Memo to Nic: When prepping for *Superman Reborn,* there's no need to leap tall buildings in a single bound.

PHOTOGRAPH BY NIGEL PARRY/CPI

SIBLING REVELRY | THE CUSACKS

IN THE PANTHEON OF HOLLYWOOD BROTHER-SISTER ACTS, John and Joan Cusack's niche is low-voltage quirkiness. After hovering on the periphery of stardom for years, both materialized in a big way in 1997—together (in *Grosse Pointe Blank*, a film he also cowrote) and separately: John, 31, as the naive narrator in *Midnight in the Garden of Good and Evil*, and Joan, 35, as the jilted-at-the-altar fiancée in *In & Out* ("Do you know how many times I sat through *Funny Girl* for you?"). Sibling rivalry? Not a chance: John welcomed Joan's baby boy (born in June) in a big-screen way, by lending his voice to *Anastasia*. "I wanted to do something for him," John says. "It's like my little gift."

TAB HUNTRESS | TEA LEONI

SHE'S A MARY RICHARDS FOR THE CYNICAL AGE: an inexplicably single, impossibly skinny journalist—but (gasp!) one who toils for a tabloid. And while Mary's niceness never wavered, Téa Leoni's alter ego on NBC's *The Naked Truth*, Nora, is both naughty *and* nice, thanks to the 31-year-old actress' own kooky glamor (more Lemon Zinger than Earl Grey). Says NBC Entertainment president Warren Littlefield: "She's gorgeous but gawky, spirited yet elegant, beautiful yet absolutely silly and funny." Green with envy yet? Consider this: She's got something *X*-tra at home—new hubby David Duchovny. Case closed.

PHOTOGRAPH BY MICHAEL GRECCO

ABSOLUTELY FABULOUS
RUPERT EVERETT

HE'S MORE LIKE Cary Grant than Cary Grant himself: tall, dark, handsome—and oh so debonair, darling. So it should have come as no surprise that 38-year-old British import Rupert Everett ended up stealing the sophisticated comedy *My Best Friend's Wedding* right out from under Julia Roberts' pretty little nose. "My part definitely grew as the film kept going," the openly gay Everett said of his surprise Stateside success. In fact, the film was reshot to beef up Everett's role as Roberts' food-critic confidant after test audiences said they wanted a second helping of the actor. "It was great," he said. "Never happened to me before."

big

MOMENTS

From the day she stepped out of London's St. Paul's Cathedral as a princess in July 1981, her eyes shyly downcast to avert the gawkers' gaze, Diana had captivated our interest, a global obsession that reached its apogee after her sudden death in a Paris car accident on Aug. 31. Though not, strictly speaking, an entertainer, Princess Diana, one of the most photographed women in the world, was a celebrity of the first rank, and stars from the entertainment biz clearly considered her family, judging by Tom Cruise's and Elizabeth Taylor's rages against paparazzi excess and Elton John's undeniably anguished tribute, "Candle in the Wind." Diana's death also made manifest the power of the media to create a shared experience, whether it was the more than 33 million Americans who set their alarm clocks to rise before dawn to view the Saturday cortege, the throngs of London mourners who crowded in front of a giant video screen in Hyde Park to watch a broadcast of the service (right), or the reported 13 million Internet users who in the days following Diana's death visited Buckingham Palace's website.

While the forlorn fascination with the passing of the Princess of Wales seemed for a time to eclipse all other news, in 1997 the pop-culture world was in fact brimming with moments of heady triumph. It was a year that began with George Lucas' *Star Wars* trilogy soaring back into orbit and ended with James Cameron's $200 million *Titanic* sailing into then-uncharted cinematic waters. And it was a year that overflowed with more than the usual quota of eye-popping scandals: The divorces, the arrests, and the tabloid titillations came fast and furious. In short, it was, as Shakespeare's Clown declares in *Twelfth Night*, a year of "most brisk and giddy-paced times." —*Nancy Bilyeau*

Star Wars Redux

■ THE AGONY...

(Feb. 24) During previews for the Broadway revival of *Annie*, producers fire their 12-year-old star, Joanna Pacitti. But before you can wail "Daddy Warbucks," she's appearing on *Rosie O'Donnell* and belting out "Tomorrow" in a North Carolina production of *Annie*. Ethel Merman would be proud.

■ ...AND THE ECSTASY

(Jan. 19) Madonna achieves global domination when the Material Mom's "Don't Cry for Me"

star turn in *Evita* snags the Golden Globe for Best Actress in a Musical or Comedy. Others who get to hug Golden Globes but not Oscars: Tom Cruise, for *Jerry Maguire*, and director Milos Forman, for *The People vs. Larry Flynt*. (Jan. 31) Twenty years after Mark Hamill first burst into Carrie Fisher's Death Star cell to blurt, "I'm Luke Skywalker—I'm here to rescue you," a remastered *Star Wars* appears on 2,104 screens. It rakes in $36 million its first weekend (the ninth-largest opening ever), proving that The Force is *still* with George Lucas & Co.

(Feb. 26) Babyface, Celine Dion, Beck, Sheryl Crow, Hillary Clinton. Hillary Clinton? Yes, the First Lady wins a Grammy for her reading of *It Takes a Village*. But the most riveting moment at the ceremony itself proves to be Jewel's see-through dress. Asked about her fashion choice, she responded, "Sometimes I don't know when to have fear."

■ BRAD AND
GWYNETH WATCH

(January) The world reacts to the news that Brad Pitt is off the market: Just in time for the New Year, his publicist confirms that the young heartthrob is engaged to Gwyneth Paltrow. The two have been inseparable since costarring as young marrieds in 1995's brutal thriller *Seven*. No date is set.

■ NEW KIDS IN TOWN

(Jan. 12) *Beavis and Butt-head* mastermind Mike Judge does it again: The prime-time Texas comedy he cocreated, *King of the Hill*, debuts to critical hur-

rahs, proving an ideal follow-up to *The Simpsons*.

■ TRENDSPOTTING

(January–February) Released just before Christmas '96, the low-budget screamer *Scream* flexes serious box office muscle in the new year, effectively updating the teen slasher flick to the '90s (now we're all in on the joke, but we're scared anyhow) and laying the

groundwork for *I Know What You Did Last Summer* and *Scream 2*.

■ YOUR HONOR, MAY WE APPROACH THE BENCH?

(January) Sitcom star Tisha Campbell alleges in court papers that she suffered years of sexual harassment from her TV husband, Martin Lawrence, on the set of *Martin*. The suit is later settled out of court.

VERBATIM // "I don't know what Gloria Steinem is talking about. Larry Flynt is *not* into violence against women. He puts them in a meat grinder *as a joke*. Doesn't she have a sense of humor?"
—The People vs. Larry Flynt *producer* OLIVER STONE, *after* The New York Times *publishes a scathing Jan. 7 editorial by Steinem attacking the film*

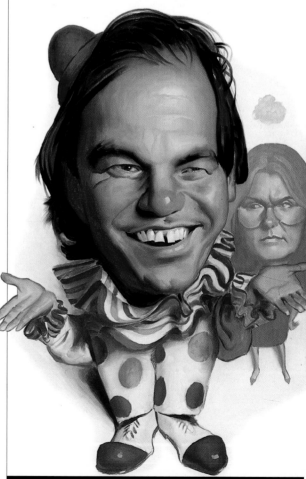

ILLUSTRATION BY DANIEL ADEL

CHANGING OF THE GUARD

(Jan. 3) **After 15 years, Bryant Gumbel retires from his spot as *Today*'s cohost and resident grouch, choking back tears on a bon voyage special—and officially making way for homefront heart-throb Matt Lauer.**

■ MURMURS OF THE HEART

(February) A relationship that lasted 15 years (and produced one son, Redmond) ends when Ryan O'Neal, 55, and Farrah Fawcett, 50, announce they're separating.

(Feb. 13) Debbie Rowe, Michael Jackson's second wife, delivers Prince Michael Joseph Jackson Jr. The proud papa reportedly sells pictures of his sleeping son to the tabloids for more than $2 million—but also informed the *National Enquirer*, "I want my son to live a normal life."

■ ADVERSITIES

(Jan. 16) Bill Cosby's 27-year-old son, Ennis, is fatally shot after pulling off a freeway in Los Angeles to fix a flat on his Mercedes. In March, 18-year-old Michael Markhasev is arrested and charged with the killing. He pleads not guilty.

caught the public's eye in December 1996.

■ CHANGING OF THE GUARD
(April 9) Twelve years after pioneering the Seattle grunge sound, Soundgarden announce their breakup. The same month, the Chemical Brothers release an acclaimed second album, *Dig Your Own Hole*. Grunge is dead. Long live...electronica?

(March 6) Whoopi Goldberg replaces Nathan Lane in the Broadway revival of *A Funny Thing Happened on the Way to the Forum*, throwing in a few coy references to her hot-and-heavy offstage relationship with Frank Langella, such as "What am I gonna do with that old white man?"

■ NEW KIDS ON THE BLOCK
(April 4) It looked like just another low-budget film about a quirky Gen-X couple, but *Chasing Amy*, directed by Kevin Smith (*Clerks*), lingers in theaters long after most other indie flicks have come and gone, earning plaudits for costars Joey Lauren Adams and Ben Affleck. Adams is later nominated for a Golden Globe for Best Musical or Comedy Actress;

Affleck will costar with Bruce Willis in 1998's big budget *Armageddon*.

■ MURMURS OF THE HEART
(March 27) Parker Stevenson, 44, files for divorce from Kirstie Alley, 42, after 13 years of giving her "the big one." But there's a silver lining: At least she'll be able to draw on firsthand experience in playing the role of a seriously dissed wife on NBC's *Veronica's Closet*.

(April 11) Three weeks after Pietra Thornton plants a well-photographed ecstatic kiss on her husband, screenwriter-director Billy

Helfgott Rachs

■ THE AGONY...
(March 4) It's not the kind of attention the classical-music world craves: When *Shine* inspiration David Helfgott goes on his first North American tour, critics bemoan his performances, saying the troubled former prodigy plays incoherently and is being exploited. Not that the critics' quibbles matter to many of his fans. One admits, "I can't even pronounce Rach...Rach..." That's Rachmaninoff, dear.

■ ...AND THE ECSTASY
(April 3) Joni Mitchell, 53, confirms that she has found the daughter she gave up for adoption 32 years ago. Her long search

VERBATIM / / "The best environment is when everybody hates you."
—HOWARD STERN (*whose surprisingly well-reviewed biopic,* Private Parts, *opens at No. 1 on March 7), explaining what fuels his on-air fun*

ILLUSTRATION BY DANIEL ADEL

Bob, at the Oscars, she sues for divorce and later claims "physical violence" in court papers—which the *Sling Blade* star denies. The couple, married four years, have two children. Pietra later poses nude for *Playboy*, telling Liz Smith, "I want people to notice me and hear my message." (April 19) The love-love match between Brooke Shields, 31, and Andre Agassi, 26, leads to the al-

tar in Pebble Beach, Calif. On the same day, Chris O'Donnell, 26, weds his longtime girlfriend, kindergarten teacher Caroline Fentress, 24, in Washington, D.C. (April) Word spreads that Shoshanna Lonstein, 21, and Jerry Seinfeld, 43, have split after a four-year relationship, and she plans to return to New York City. Not that there's anything wrong with that.

(March 17) Adrienne Barbeau, of *Maude* fame, gives birth to identical twins at age 51.

■ YOUR HONOR, MAY WE APPROACH THE BENCH?
(April 3) Mommy Culkin (Patricia Brentrup) won't have to be home alone after all: She wins custody of Macaulay, 16, and four of his six siblings from ex-mate Kit Culkin, after a bitter court battle.

■ BRAD AND GWYNETH WATCH
Pitt shows up for the Manhattan premiere of his movie *The Devil's Own* glued to Paltrow, their hair dyed and cut to match. Gwyneth freely admits she turned down the to-die-for role of Emma Peel in *The Avengers* for love: She just couldn't tolerate a four-month separation from Brad.

GOODING PLENTY

(March 24) What was it like to win Best Supporting Actor for *Jerry Maguire*? "Refreshing"—just like Gatorade, Cuba Gooding Jr. tells reporters. Apart from the actor's winning touchdown, *The English Patient* exerts a stranglehold on the Oscars (Best Picture, Best Director, Best Supporting Actress, etc.)—so much so that *Evita* winner Andrew Lloyd Webber gushes, "Thank heavens there wasn't a song in *The English Patient*."

MAY
JUNE

ID NO. **974254** DATE **05:27:97**
ARLINGTON COUNTY POLICE

■ **THE AGONY...**

(May) After pictures of hubby Frank's hotel nooky with an ex–flight attendant hit the tabs, Kathie Lee Gifford, the poster girl for family values, first goes into denial, then issues, with the Giff, a public plea for privacy. When the dust settles, she's sporting a tartier look.

(May 2) Just another world-famous actor offering a West Hollywood hooker a lift home in the wee hours of the morning. That's Eddie Murphy's Good Samaritan explanation after police stop his car to question his passenger, a 20-year-old transsexual who is wanted on an outstanding warrant (and will later be sentenced to 90 days in jail). Murphy might have been better off saying he was doing research for *Beverly Hills Cop IV*.

(May 22) Trouble in 'toonville. A carrot-toting Bugs Bunny (below left) appears on a U.S. postage stamp—the first animated character to be so honored—prompting some philatelic purists to rage against the hare-raising desecration. Lighten up—it could have been the Tasmanian Devil.

(May 19) What can you say about a 55-year-old sportscaster who loved basketball, hockey, and backbiting? Marv Albert (left) is indicted on sex-assault charges. (He will plead guilty to a lesser charge at his September trial and be fired by NBC.) Amid the claims and counterclaims about what happened in that Virginia hotel room, one thing is certain: It was no love story.

─────────

■ **...AND THE ECSTASY**

(May) After four months of tense negotiations, the cast of *Seinfeld* finalizes a deal for the 1997–1998 season's salaries: Jerry will earn $1 million per episode, while Jason Alexander, Julia Louis-Dreyfus, and Michael Richards will each get $600,000 (up from $150,000). That should just about cover the cost of lunch at Monk's Coffee Shop until, oh...about the year 2250.

(May 18–19) What fare do viewers hunger for most at sweeps time? Is it (a) a terrifying ghost story, (b) a Mafia-meets-Hollywood crime drama, or (c) a classical epic about a Greek's 10-year journey home to his wife after the Trojan War? You win if you picked (c), NBC's *The Odyssey*. The Homeric

VERBATIM // "To have the music loved so *much* and then rejected out of hand within a decade...your family thinks it's over for you. You're no longer going to be a pop star: 'What are you gonna do *now*, Dad?'"

—BARRY GIBB, 50, on the perils of being a Bee Gee. (Weep not: On May 6, he and his brothers prove they're stayin' alive when they're inducted into the Rock and Roll Hall of Fame.)

ILLUSTRATION BY DANIEL ADEL

miniseries—starring Armand Assante, Bernadette Peters, and Vanessa Williams—outscores such other big guns as *Stephen King's The Shining* and *Mario Puzo's The Last Don*. Can *The Iliad* be far behind?

■ MURMURS
OF THE HEART
(May 6) The Naked Troth: *The X-Files'* David Duchovny, 36, weds Téa Leoni, 31, and before long makes it known that he wants his spooky Fox series moved from Vancouver to L.A. so that he can be nearer to the missus. (May) Spike Lee, 40, and

his wife, Tonya, 31, have a second child, Jackson Lewis Lee. Julia Louis-Dreyfus, 36, and hubby Brad Hall also welcome a boy: Charles.

■ YOUR HONOR, MAY WE APPROACH THE BENCH?
(May 27) An L.A. judge rules in favor of Pamela Lee, 29, in a breach-of-contract suit involving the Showtime movie *Hello, She Lied*. The *Playboy* centerfold–turned–*Baywatch* babe said she backed out of the film after realizing the script called for sex scenes. What—did she think she was going to play Ophelia?

■ BRAD AND
GWYNETH WATCH
(June) Pitt's publicist drops the bomb: The golden couple is no more. Vague explanations for the breakup—"It wasn't over any one thing"—abound. What complicates Pitt's life even more

is the not-very-pleasant revelation that the real-life historical character he plays in the fall release *Seven Years in Tibet* has admitted to being a member of Adolf Hitler's notorious SS before he met up with the Dalai Lama.

WE JUST DIDN'T SEE IT COMING
(JUNE 6) We never thought she was a candidate for Mensa or anything, but still, Farrah Fawcett's incoherent dithering on the *Late Show With David Letterman* proves a shocker. Afterward, Fawcett denies rumors of drug use. Gallantly taking the blame, her ex-manager said he had advised her to "act like Marilyn Monroe." Next time, Farrah, go with Bette Davis.

JULY AUGUST

Flowers for Versace

■ THE AGONY...
(July 31) There's an old showbiz saying: Never work with kids or animals. To that list, Penny Marshall might add...Muppets. At a publicity fashion show for Kmart's new *Sesame Street* line, Marshall loses her balance on the runway, tearing off Big Bird's wing in front of a horrified crowd that includes many kids. Not to worry, the bird reassures

the crowd—*and* the stunned director—"it'll grow back."

■ ...AND THE ECSTASY
(Aug. 12) It's an all-out Mac attack: With a reunion concert on MTV, a new album, and a 40-city tour, Mick Fleetwood's seminal '70s band has baby boomers fondly recalling the days when *Rumours* never left their turntable. When a slimmed-down Stevie Nicks twirls across the stage, Lindsey Buckingham voices inner torment, and Christine McVie sings perfect pitches, it feels as if we've still got Jimmy Carter in the White House.
(July–August) The actor generating the summer's highest-voltage buzz hasn't gotten this much critical attention (well, *positive* critical attention, anyway) since he rode a long-barreled motorcycle and called himself Captain America. The 57-year-old Peter Fonda plays a stoic beekeeper in *Ulee's Gold* who, when provoked, is not afraid to sting.

■ NEW KIDS
ON THE BLOCK
(Aug. 13) "Oh, my God, they killed Kenny"—that's the signature line for *South Park*, the animated breakout hit that debuts on Comedy Central to instant culthood. See 8-year-old Kenny impaled! Watch him

get trampled! shot! microwaved! pecked to death by mutant turkeys! This one makes *Ren & Stimpy* look like *Touched by an Angel*.

■ MURMURS
OF THE HEART
(July 26) *Titanic* director James Cameron, 42, marries his *Terminator 2* leading lady, Linda Hamilton, 40. Good news: The wedding goes over budget by only a few gazillion bucks.
(July 29) Will the Cable Guy become the Lonely Guy? After just nine months of marriage, Lauren Holly, 33, files for divorce from Jim Carrey, 35, citing irreconcilable differences. On the same day, *Party of Five*'s Neve Campbell, 23, announces she's once again a party of one, separating from husband Jeff Colt, 29, after two and a half years of marriage.
(July 10) Pretender Chrissie Hynde, 45, weds Colombian artist Lucho Brieva, 32, in London.
(Aug. 2) *Frasier*'s Kelsey Grammer, 42, marries film

VERBATIM // "The first thing that crossed my mind was to bite him back."
—EVANDER HOLYFIELD *on the July 3* Late Show With David Letterman, *reflecting on the Mike Tyson chomp heard round the world—and seen by 2 million people on pay per view*

ILLUSTRATION BY DANIEL ADEL

student Camille Donatacci, 28, in Malibu. It's his third marriage.

■ YOUR HONOR, MAY WE APPROACH THE BENCH? (Aug. 11) We're accustomed to Charlie Sheen as chronic headline fodder, but Christian Slater? The 27-year-old actor and Jack Nicholson wannabe is arrested at a party in Los Angeles; police later say that Slater, who has had brushes with the law before, punched his girlfriend and then tussled with the fellow who came to her defense. The bad-boy behavior earns Slater 90 days in the pokey, a sentence his lawyer asked to have reduced. Slater said of the problems that led to his legal woes, "As much praise as people give...there's still a voice in our heads that tells us 'You suck.'"

■ BRAD AND GWYNETH WATCH (July 14) Is there anything worse than intimate photos surfacing while you're in the throes of romance? Absolutely—having the photos achieve widespread circulation *after* the breakup. Pitt sues *Playgirl* for invasion of privacy and other complaints after the magazine publishes nude photos of him and Paltrow taken in 1995 in St. Bart's without their knowledge. Pitt's lawyers convince a judge to order *Playgirl* to pull all of the offending copies from the newsstands. The final resolution was still pending at year's end.

■ ADVERSITIES (July 15) The shooting death of designer Gianni Versace, 50, in Miami Beach sends shock waves through not only fashion circles but the entire entertainment world (see obituary in Bowing Out). Eight days later, Andrew Cunanan, the prime suspect, is found dead in a Miami houseboat, an apparent suicide.

BROOKS' BROTHERS
(AUG. 7) Call it Thursday in the Park With Garth. Some 250,000 people—many sporting cowboy hats—stride into Central Park to see the king of country, Garth Brooks. Though he kicks off the HBO concert with the cry "Let's raise some hell!" the NYPD makes just five arrests, mostly for minor offenses.

tion best-seller list. (Sept. 17) After 15 years of "making the dough-nuts," Fred (in reality, 73-year-old actor Michael Vale) retires as the well-loved TV commercial pitchman for Dunkin' Donuts. "We are ready to focus more on the cus-tomers' experience with our products," explains a Dunkin' spokesperson.

■ ...AND THE ECSTASY (September) Deepak Chopra, move over. The new spiritual movement that has Hollywood in thrall is kabbalah, a mys-tic branch of Judaism. Students include Madon-na, Courtney Love, Barbra Streisand, and Elizabeth Taylor. Coming soon to a cineplex near you: *Torah! Torah! Torah!*

■ NEW KID ON THE BLOCK (Sept. 3) Not since Capt. James T. Kirk tumbled a bevy of beehived cosmic babes in the '60s has there been this much va-voom in space. Volup-tuous Jeri Ryan joins the cast of *Star Trek: Voyager* as part-Borg character Seven of Nine. Sniffs se-ries regular Robert Picar-do: "The concept [seemed to be] to put a female on who was *so* attrac-tive, a guy chan-nel-surfing would hit on *Voyager*... and he would spend the rest of the night drooling." You got it, pal.

■ CHANGING OF THE GUARD (Sept. 5) Maybe there's a statute of limitations on morning cheer. Joan Lun-den bids farewell to ABC's *Good Morning*

A Royal Pain

■ THE AGONY... (Sept. 17) Less than three weeks after Princess Di-ana's death, Kitty Kelley's dirt disher on the Wind-sors, *The Royals*, hits bookstores. Most stom-ach-churning moment: Kelley's tearful lament that she tried unsuccess-fully to get the book de-layed ("I'm sick that it's coming out now"). Next-worst moment: The book debuts at No. 1 on the *Publishers Weekly* nonfic-

America after 17 years. Next up: fresh face (and Joan clone) Lisa McRee.

■ BRAD AND GWYNETH WATCH (September–October) Pal-trow must have been his lucky charm. Pitt's fall movie *Seven Years in Tibet* stumbles at the box of-fice, while a beaming Gwyneth makes the rounds at events like the

Boogie Nights premiere, often with fellow Gen-X gal pal Winona Ryder.

■ WE JUST DIDN'T SEE IT COMING (Sept. 11) In a move that some pundits believe is spurred on by Mel Gib-son's chest-thumping 1995 Oscar winner, *Brave-heart*, a majority of Scots vote in favor of "devolu-tion," the first step to-

VERBATIM / / "There's no safety net, and I love that. My maxim is, Risk all.... There's no more time to be afraid. I won't be young long."
—*The 29-year-old* LUCY LAWLESS, *best known for* Xena: War-rior Princess, *as she trades in her Amazon armor for Rizzo's trampy getups in the Broadway revival of* Grease!

ILLUSTRATION BY DANIEL ADEL

ward independence from England. What's next? Brainwashed government assassins bonding together over Gibson's latest, *Conspiracy Theory*?

■ MURMURS
OF THE HEART
(Sept. 12) *Star Trek: The Next Generation*'s Patrick Stewart, 57, and former *Star Trek: Voyager* producer Wendy Neuss, 39, announce their engagement. Ahead, warp factor 1.
(Sept. 5) Just because your last name is King doesn't mean you have to one-up Henry VIII. CNN's Larry King, 63, takes a sixth wife, singer Shawn Southwick, 37. The two are married in a hospital room at the UCLA Medical Center, where King was under observation for heart trouble.
(Sept. 27) Arnold Schwarzenegger, 50, and news correspondent Maria Shriver, 41, welcome their fourth child, a boy.
(Sept. 24) Another one bites the dust. *Jungle* hunk Brendan Fraser, 28, announces his engagement to former actress Afton Smith, 30.

■ YOUR HONOR, MAY WE APPROACH THE BENCH?
(Sept. 9) It sure isn't the first celebrity lawsuit against the *National Enquirer*, but it has to be one of the oddest. Christie Brinkley, 43, files a $42 million defamation suit, alleging the *Enquirer* published libelous stories, including one saying she ordered "cops to shoot a cow that mooed at her while she was playing tennis." At year-end, a decision was pending about the *Enquirer*'s motion to have the case dismissed.
(Sept. 12) Former *Beverly Hills, 90210* star Shannen Doherty, 26, is sentenced to counseling and two years' probation after she pleads no contest to a vandalism charge stemming from an argument outside a bar that culminated in Doherty's smashing a beer bottle on a car window. Looks like grounding her didn't do the trick.

OH, BROTHERS
(SEPT. 14) The sibling shrink stars of *Frasier*, David Hyde Pierce and Kelsey Grammer, rejoice after the show wins its fourth consecutive Emmy award for Outstanding Comedy Series (and yes, that's Bruce Willis applauding). The night's biggest surprise: *Law & Order* wins for Outstanding Drama Series on its sixth try.

Sein-ing Off

■ THE AGONY...
(Dec. 26) It's tough to say who is hit harder by the news that 1997–98 is the last season for *Seinfeld*—the bereaved fans or the anguished NBC execs who will have one huge hole to fill on Thursdays. The news affects other folks in different ways: Al Yeganeh, the Manhattan soup czar immortalized in the "Soup Nazi" episode, reportedly becomes enraged when a radio reporter shows up at his stand and asks Yeganeh to say on the air, "No soup for you!" According to one newspaper story, he chased the reporter away, shouting "Get out!"

■ ...AND THE ECSTASY
(Nov. 2) We'll never grow tired of those glass slippers. A TV version of *Cinderella* starring Brandy, Whitney Houston, Whoopi Goldberg, and Jason Alexander scores huge ratings, giving ABC its best Sunday-night numbers in more than a decade.

■ WE JUST DIDN'T SEE IT COMING
(Dec. 23) Do you find that more than 20 years later, "Dancing Queen" is still occupying valuable space in your cerebral cortex? Well, brace yourself. The music of ABBA, the Swedish band responsible for such immortal pop-lite '70s hits as "Knowing Me, Knowing You" and "Take a Chance on Me," is rumored to be the subject for an upcoming stage musical, expected to open in London in 1999.

■ BRAD AND GWYNETH WATCH
(November–December) Is there life after Brad Pitt? Sure, there is—if you're Gwyneth Paltrow. Gossip columns report that the lanky beauty is keeping company with *Chasing Amy* star Ben Affleck. As for Pitt, he's still playing it cool with his love life, but his career looks hotter than ever: He's reportedly earning $17.5 million for 1998's *Meet Joe Black*. After finishing that film, he tells *Interview*, he may take a break: "The thing about art is that you can't keep churning it out."

■ MURMURS OF THE HEART
(Nov. 10) Model Darcy La-Pier, 31, files court papers accusing actor husband Jean-Claude Van Damme, 37, of spousal abuse and drug-fueled mood swings. The charges surface in the *Timecop*'s divorce action against LaPier. Van Damme and LaPier are divorce-court regulars; they have split up and reconciled numer-

VERBATIM / / "I've built a career in which fear doesn't exist. If nothing else, I think I've proven that.... I mean, if I was scared, I wouldn't have done *Pulp Fiction* the way I did, okay? I would have cast Daniel Day-Lewis instead of John Travolta."
—*Director* QUENTIN TARANTINO, 34, *who just might get a chance to demonstrate his fearlessness in court, thanks to a $5 million assault-and-battery suit filed on Nov. 14 by producer Don Murphy, who says Tarantino attacked him in a West Hollywood restaurant Oct. 22 and then boasted of his attack on* The Keenen Ivory Wayans Show

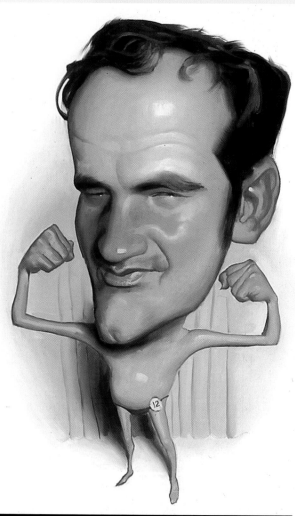

ILLUSTRATION BY DANIEL ADEL

ous times in the past. (Dec. 31) Red-hot actor Will Smith, 29, weds actress Jada Pinkett, 26; they're expecting a child in the summer.

Bringing up babies: On Nov. 10, Lois Lane/Bond girl Teri Hatcher, 32, and her actor husband, Jon Tenney, 35, have a girl, Emerson Rose. On Dec. 9, Mick Jagger, 54, and his wife, Jerry Hall, 41, welcome their fourth child, Gabriel Luke Beauregard. And on Dec. 29, Pamela Lee, 30, gives birth to her second son with rocker Tommy Lee, Dylan Jagger. (Memo to Pamela and Tommy: On this occasion, a video camera *would* have been appropriate.)

■ YOUR HONOR, MAY WE APPROACH THE BENCH? (Nov. 20) Martha's to-do list for the day: "Finalize menu for Thanksgiving dinner for 24. Plant chrysanthemums. Refinish antique chair. Sue tabloid." Martha Stewart, 56, files a libel suit against the *National Enquirer*, seeking more than $10 million for a September story headlined "Martha Stewart Mentally Ill." Stewart says the story isn't true; the *Enquirer* says it is "confident" in its story.

(Dec. 8) Robert Downey Jr. is sentenced to 180 days in the L.A. County Jail for violating probation. In August 1996 the actor had pleaded no contest to charges that included cocaine and heroin possession, carrying a concealed weapon, and driving under the influence, and had been given probation. At Downey's sentencing, Judge Lawrence Mira says, "It may be the very business you are in that is conducive to you continuing this lifestyle."

(Dec. 12) Autumn Jackson, 23, who had threatened to go to the tabs with the story that she was Bill Cosby's daughter unless she was paid $40 million, gets 26 months in prison for extortion. "I want to apologize to the court and to Mr. Cosby for the...embarrassment I caused him," Jackson said at her sentencing. Cosby has denied being Jackson's father.

(Dec. 22) Hell hath no fury like a pregnant woman scorned. Actress Hunter Tylo is awarded nearly $5 million in damages in a lawsuit against Spelling Entertainment. Tylo was hired to portray a sexy man-stealing vixen on *Melrose Place* (as if there were a shortage) and said she was fired after telling producers about her pregnancy. Lawyers for Aaron Spelling's production company are appealing.

PARIS MATCH

(DEC. 23) Oh, to be in Paris in the wintertime...with the daughter of your ex-girlfriend. Woody Allen, 62, marries Soon-Yi Previn, 27—the adopted daughter of onetime Allen muse Mia Farrow—in Venice, and the couple travel to Paris afterward. Allen's spokesperson denies published reports that he is writing a script for a play in which his bride will appear. So it looks like we won't be seeing *Hannah and Her Daughters*.

"PAY NO ATTENTION TO THAT MAN BEHIND THE CURTAIN!" bellowed the Wizard to Dorothy as she spotted the flustered fellow creating the illusion of the fearsome Oz. Yet who can resist occasionally sneaking a peek to discover who's really pulling life's illusory strings? We all enjoy the thrill of glimpsing a performer before the camera rolls to see if his private face matches his celluloid one. The pictures on the following pages capture just such moments behind the scenes of some of the most talked-about films, TV shows, and music and book tours of 1997, whether it's the cast of *ER* dissolving into laughter before the nerve-racking live episode that opened their fall season, Steven Spielberg whispering direction into the scaly ear of one of his *Lost World* dino stars, or Frank McCourt tearing away from his *Angela's Ashes* promotional duties to visit a misty Irish graveyard.

LIAR'S CLUB

PLAYING A DUPLICITOUS lawyer who's forced to tell the whole truth and nothing but the truth for 24 hours, Jim Carrey pushed his double-jointed derring-do to new heights in *Liar Liar*. The film's $181 million box office take made fibbers out of those who said *The Cable Guy* had cross-wired the comic's winning streak—so don't expect a discount on his $20 million asking price. "I mean, there's other carbon-based life-forms out there that make the same money I do," Carrey told one interviewer. "I'd be a stupid idiot if I took less when I could get more." One thing he's *not* is dumb. Or dumber.

Behind {the} Scenes

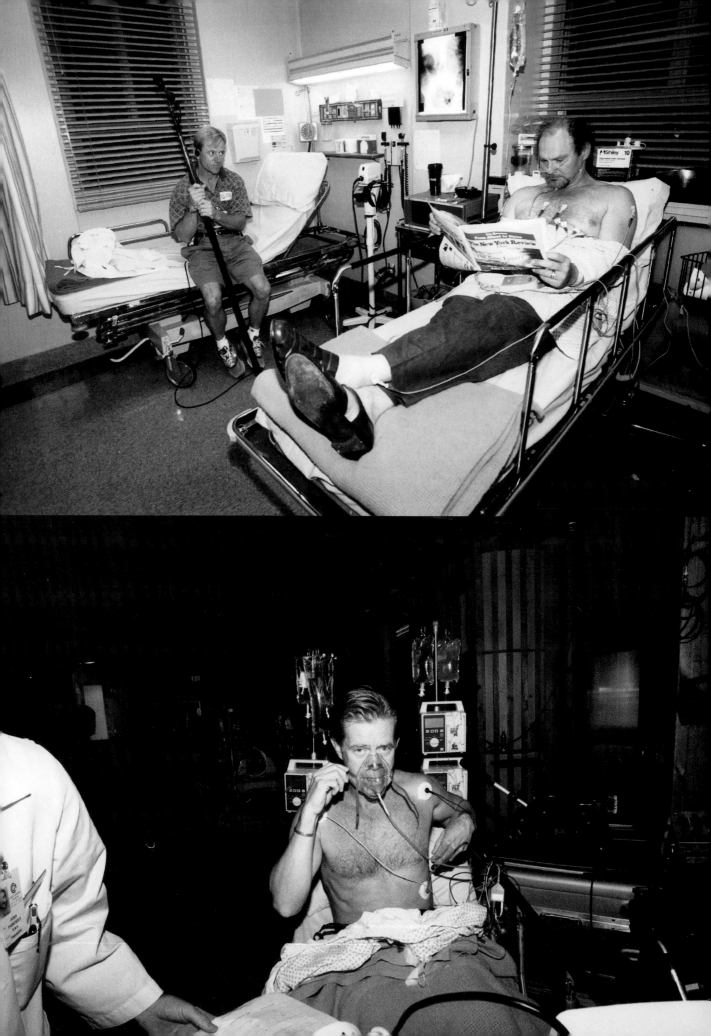

WHAT'S UP, DOCS?

TALK ABOUT A HIGH-RISK OPERATION. Inspired by the dangerous immediacy of '50s dramas like *Playhouse 90*, stars George Clooney and Anthony Edwards of TV's top-rated *ER* proposed that the season opener be a live telecast. (Make that *two* live broadcasts, one for each coast.) Logistics were plotted with surgical precision: Eleven cameras covered the 27-room set, which teemed with more than 100 people, many of the backstage crew disguised on air in scrubs. "I'm petrified," Julianna Margulies confessed before the adrenaline-charged dress rehearsal, but the cast—(above, left to right) Laura Innes, Edwards, Margulies, Clooney, Eriq La Salle, and Noah Wyle, along with guest star Sherman Howard (top left) and recurring star William H. Macy (left)—pulled through. Still, aren't the flubs why we watch? In a scene in which Dr. Ross examined a wailing baby girl, the infant used for the East Coast version howled; the West Coast's kid didn't utter a peep. Call her agent—*stat!*

PHOTOGRAPHS BY LARA JO REGAN/GAMMA-LIAISON

| SHINE OF THE TIMES

YOU'RE A FAMOUS AUTHOR and you don't like the way a famous director has interpreted one of your best-sellers—what do you do? If you're Stephen King, you remake it yourself. Horrified by the liberties director Stanley Kubrick and Jack ("*Heeeere's Johnny!*") Nicholson took with the 1980 film *The Shining*, King made sure he ruled when ABC remade his horror classic into a May sweeps miniseries. As executive producer—and as the film's ghostly hotel bandleader—King (far right, in full makeup) got cheeky with star Steven Weber, proving that all work and no play does not, after all, make for dull boys.

PHOTOGRAPH BY ANTONIN KRATOCHVIL/SABA

DIRECT AND TO THE POINT

"I GET A GUT FEELING," said first-time director Christopher Reeve on the set of HBO's *In the Gloaming,* "and that's all I'm going on." Reeve, paralyzed since a 1995 riding accident (and supported, above, by wife Dana and son Will), relied on TV monitors and an intercom system to run the show. "I'm just beginning, and I think trusting your instincts is a good place to start." The critics agreed: The drama, about a family coping with a son's struggle with AIDS, was nominated for five Emmys. Steven Spielberg (right, directing one of his prehistoric stars) knows a thing or two about instincts too—at least commercial ones. His *Jurassic Park* sequel, *The Lost World,* was one of the summer's biggest hits, stomping most of its competitors at the box office with a $227 million take. Said Spielberg of his return to the director's chair after a three-year absence: "I didn't want to do a serious movie after *Schindler's List.*" He succeeded.

JENNY-FLECTION

SHE AIN'T EXACTLY GONNA SWEEP the Emmys, but how many ex-Playmates are singled out to star in their own sitcom four years after setting foot in Hollywood? Pinup-turned-cutup Jenny McCarthy, 25, known mostly for her goofy mugging and over-the-top bathroom humor on MTV, was handed a fall NBC show with the hope that she could become the next Lucy (albeit with sex appeal)—a sort of Jim Carrey with boobs. For her part, McCarthy said she just wanted to play a role where she could "sit down and have a normal conversation. Still my personality, but not, you know, throwing up on camera."

PHOTOGRAPH BY MARISSA ROTH

ALIENATION AND AFFECTION

BRIDGET LOVED BERNIE. Cher skewered Sonny. Oscar irked Felix. And now we have the '90s answer to odd coupledom: *Dharma & Greg* (left), one of the breakout rookie hits of the fall TV season. Clever and cornball in equal measures, *D&G* chronicles the culture-shock marriage of granola-eating do-gooder Dharma Finkelstein (Jenna Elfman) and buttoned-down WASP lawyer Greg Montgomery (Thomas Gibson). Will success spoil the sitcom sweethearts? Not necessarily—just ask *3rd Rock From the Sun* star John Lithgow (above), who has scored two consecutive Emmys as the leader of an all-in-good-fun alien insurrection: "I cluster [my Emmys] on top of a big credenza in my dressing room. And up there with my awards, I have a great big statue of Groucho Marx, just to put everything in perspective."

PHOTOGRAPHS BY LARA JO REGAN/GAMMA-LIAISON

GIRLS' NIGHTS OUT

JUST DON'T CALL IT GAL-APALLOOZA. When Canadian songstress Sarah McLachlan decided to launch a 1997 summer-music tour, she had one rule: women only. As it turns out, that's what everyone wanted to hear: The show—dubbed Lilith Fair in honor of a biblical feminist symbol and starring, among others, Tracy Chapman, Jewel, McLachlan, Suzanne Vega, and Paula Cole (grouped at left, l. to r.)—was one of the year's biggest hits. Whether it was the intensely personal pop of Cole, performing in Arizona (top left), or the cerebral musings of Vega, emerging from her trailer in Orange County, Calif. (above), the tour drew a rapt response, raking in close to $16 million in more than 30 cities. Yet these women claimed to be fueled by more than competitive juices. "This is not about being better than something else," McLachlan said. "It's celebrating what we are—the fact that we've finally come into a time where women can be heard and respected and loved for what they say." They are women—hear them roar.

STRANGE BEDFELLOWS

SURE, *POLITICALLY INCORRECT* MADE THE JUMP from sophisticated New York to glitzy L.A. But could the talk show graduate from Comedy Central to the network big leagues a year later? That's what skeptics wondered about Bill Maher's self-described "cocktail party." But *PI* has more than survived—it has thrived, filling ABC's night-owl slot and attracting a higher-profile pool of guests, including *Hustler* honcho Larry Flynt (above). Another performer who busted out in 1997 was Helena Bonham Carter, who slipped her corset (and her buttoned-down image) in *The Wings of the Dove*. The actress (right), sharing a modern moment with director Iain Softley, oozed sensuality as an upper-class schemer torn between love of man and money. What drew Carter to the Henry James heroine? "There's nothing innocent about her *whatsoever*."

TO EIRE IS DIVINE

EVIDENTLY, YOU *CAN* go home again. When 67-year-old author Frank McCourt returned in 1997 to Limerick, Ireland, the poor-as-church-mice setting of his childhood memoir, *Angela's Ashes*, he was a certified literary lion. But while his Pulitzer-winning best-seller had been the toast of every book signing in America (spawning deals for a literary sequel *and* a film version), in some quarters of Limerick the reception for McCourt was as chilly as a fresh draft of Guinness. "Some people are saying I made all the suffering up," the author told one interviewer. "I wish I did. My sister and two brothers wouldn't have died as children."

Style

The looks that dared to dazzle

{1997}

BY DEGEN PENER

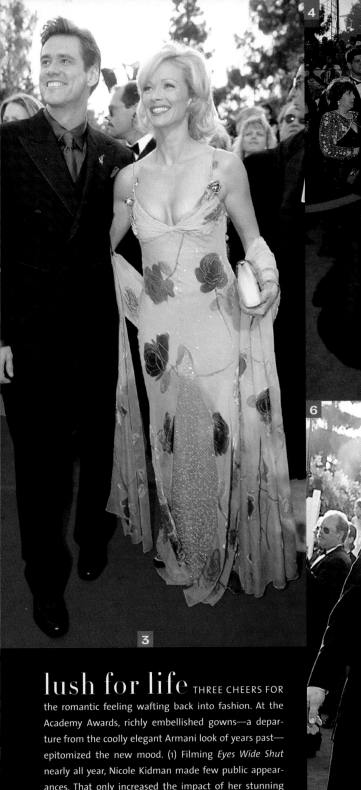

lush for life

THREE CHEERS FOR the romantic feeling wafting back into fashion. At the Academy Awards, richly embellished gowns—a departure from the coolly elegant Armani look of years past—epitomized the new mood. (1) Filming *Eyes Wide Shut* nearly all year, Nicole Kidman made few public appearances. That only increased the impact of her stunning presence at the Oscars, alongside husband Tom Cruise, in an embroidered Dior gown by John Galliano. (2) *The English Patient*'s Juliette Binoche had no trouble collaring a win for Best Supporting Actress in her bold Sophie Sitbon dress. (3) Four months before filing for divorce, Lauren Holly, in flowery Valentino, seemed the perfect match for Jim Carrey. (4) Lacroix, sweetie! *The English Patient*'s Kristin Scott Thomas would be the envy of Patsy and Edina in a sweeping number by the French couturier. (5) Claire Danes wasn't feeling romantic, just blue. But her cashmere top with skirt was the perfect mix of teenage style and awards-show glitz. (6) Susan Sarandon, with Tim Robbins, gave back in a gold velvet gown by Donna Karan.

glitz and glory COMPARED WITH THE MOVIE WORLD, TV MAY BE CONSIDERED LOW-KEY.

But it's not necessarily less gorgeous, as the Emmys proved last September. (1) *Frasier*'s Jane Leeves made a slit decision in a Halston Signature gown by Randolph Duke. (2) *Touched by an Angel*'s Roma Downey, in Pamela Dennis, bustled down the red carpet. (3) *Mad About You*'s Helen Hunt, winner for Best Actress in a Comedy, looked as good as it gets in a silver Laurél. (4) Arriving with escort Rod Rowland, *The X-Files*' Gillian Anderson, winner for Best Actress in a Drama, was well trained in a gown by Felicia Farrar. (5) *Cybill*'s Christine Baranski, in Robert Turturici, brought up the rear in the evening's parade of simply elegant dresses.

1

2

flower power CELEBS TURNED OVER A NEW LEAF BY EMBRACING FASHION'S RAGE FOR ALL THINGS

animal (in the form of fashionably phony fur) and vegetable. (1) Gwyneth Paltrow, at the premiere of her film *Hard Eight*, looked trim in a fur-collared floral coat by Dolce & Gabbana. (2) Jada Pinkett, with Will Smith, had her fur up at the 1997 MTV Video Music Awards. (3) In Cannes, Demi Moore got pelted in dyed blue Dolce & Gabbana. (4) "Madam, I'm Adam," says Jim Carrey, at the VH1 Fashion Awards. (5) Prada's vine designs clung to Jennifer Lopez at the Independent Spirit Awards. (6) Fiona Apple bloomed at the Grammys. What next—topiary gowns?

6

5

4

3

what a heel

DESPITE THE FOOT WOES THEY CAN cause, vertiginous pumps, such as Gucci's steel-spiked version (left), kicked their way back into style. They gave an extra boost, sometimes as much as four or five inches, to celebrities like Courtney Love (right), in Versace by Donatella, at the VH1 Fashion Awards.

boogie nights AT THE 1997

MTV Video Music Awards in September, subtlety was the real fashion victim. (1) Raunchy rapper Busta Rhymes looked as if he were preparing to curtsy. (2) Rappers Lisa "Left Eye" Lopes, Angie Martinez, Lil' Kim, Da Brat, and Missy Elliott revived gladiator style, to illin' effect. (3) The Spice Girls, despite their vocally strained live performance, made a more fashionable five. (4) Don't speak about Gwen Stefani's style tribute to *Star Trek*. At least she didn't wear a diaper on stage like fellow No Doubt member Adrian Young. (5) No over-the-top *Evita* gowns for Madonna: The new mom looked as if she'd just come from dropping off daughter Lourdes at a Catholic girls' school. (6) From thigh to midriff, presenter Mariah Carey showed off her newfound sexy side in Vera Wang. (7) Amid all this fashion insanity, Jay Kay of Jamiroquai, winner for Best Video, stole the show in his striking stovepipe hat. What a way to top off the night.

skin game

THERE'S NO BUSINESS LIKE PEEP-SHOW business. That maxim seemed to hold true all last year as celebrities bared what kind of underwear was under there. (1) At the 1997 MTV Movie Awards in Los Angeles in June, *Jerry Maguire*'s Renée Zellweger, in Giorgio Armani, and *Kiss the Girls*' Ashley Judd, in Valentino, sported lace tops. (2) Believe it or not, Ripley, a.k.a. Sigourney Weaver, delved into inner space in Dolce & Gabbana at the L.A. premiere of *Alien Resurrection*. (3) It's all coming back to haunt her now: Celine Dion may have been showing off her Grammy statue, but all eyes were on her poor choice of white underwear beneath a black see-through Ralph Lauren dress. (4) At ShoWest in Las Vegas, Winona Ryder was sensible enough to pair a slip with her transparent Prada number. (5) Toni Braxton looked in perfect racing-stripe form at the Grammys, exposing just the right amount of skin in a long-trained gown by Marc Bouwer. (6) Sheryl Crow, also at the Grammys, slipped up in a revealing outfit by Dolce & Gabbana. But if it makes her happy... (7) Singer Maxwell, at the 1997 MTV Video Music Awards, looked smooth in a barely there shirt. But no matter whether the results were revealingly sexy or unintentionally hilarious, this trend was a sheer delight.

muted beauty

MINIMAL AFFECT YIELDED maximum effect for these fashionably restrained celebs. (1) Elizabeth Hurley—in a stunning, glittery dress and her signature diamond crucifix—makes like a minx at the premiere of *Austin Powers*. (2) Kate Moss, in a demure white sheath, helps on-again, off-again boyfriend Johnny Depp get better adjusted at the Cannes International Film Festival. (3) At the premiere of her film *In Love and War*, Sandra Bullock, on the arm of Matthew McConaughey, makes glamour look effortless in a Donna Karan gown. (4) Cameron Diaz, at the premiere of *My Best Friend's Wedding*, takes the cake in a navy dress that is the epitome of elegant simplicity. (5) Michelle Pfeiffer, with Jessica Lange at the premiere of *A Thousand Acres*, puts the film's farmer's-wife frocks behind her with an elegant Giorgio Armani. Less really is more, more, more.

been there, overdone that SOME STARS ENDED UP BIG DIPPERS BY POURING ON TOO

much substance and too little style. (1) Eye shadow overshadows Fiona Apple at the VH1 Fashion Awards. (2) Kirstie Alley, stuck in *Veronica's Closet*, puts on one layer too many for the premiere of *For Richer or Poorer*. (3) Uma Thurman is anything but perfection in a silly black wig at the *Gattaca* premiere. (4) Claudia Schiffer wilts at the VH1 Fashion Awards. (5) Alicia Silverstone needs white-out at the *Batman & Robin* premiere. (6) Pamela Lee, with husband Tommy at The American Music Awards, finally finds an accessory that dwarfs her best-known assets.

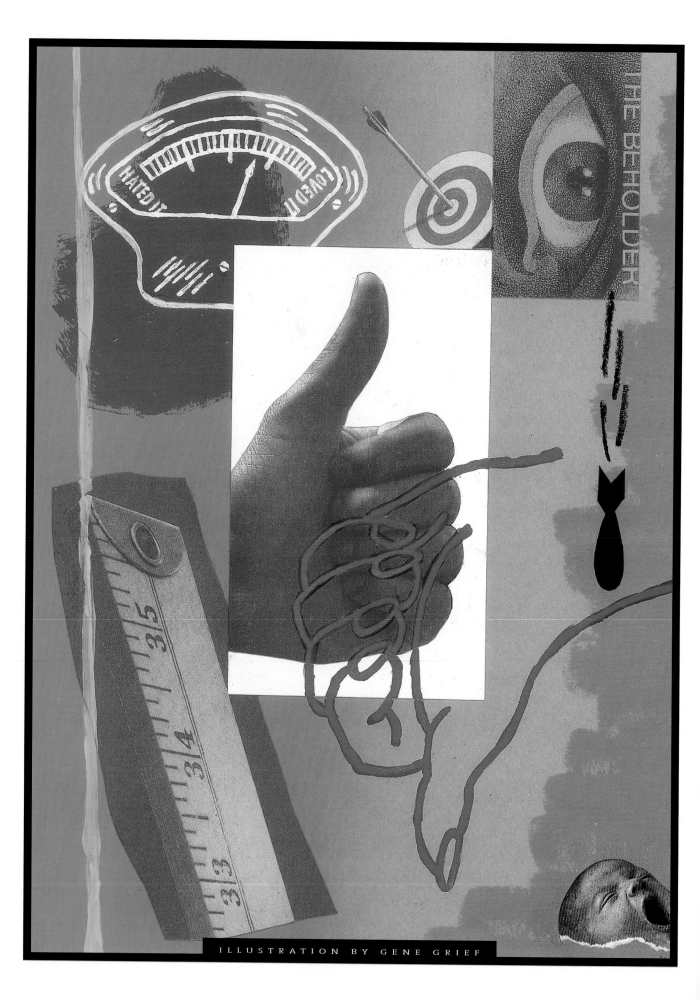

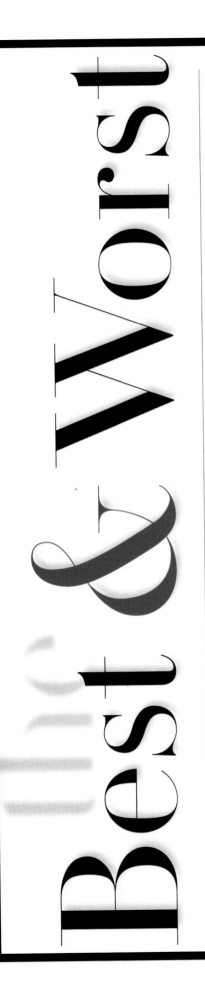

Best & Worst

ONE OF THE MADDENING IRONIES OF THE pop-culture world is that every year we hear the lament that the previous 12 months were a wasteland of stale movies, TV shows, CDs, and books, and yet every year we see a burst of exciting and original work. That was truer than ever in 1997. On our critics' lists of favorites can be found the exhilarating pleasures of *Boogie Nights* and *L.A. Confidential*, television's *King of the Hill* and *Everybody Loves Raymond*, Radiohead's album *OK Computer* and Charles Frazier's debut novel, *Cold Mountain*, the long-in-coming video *Céline and Julie Go Boating* and the eagerly awaited *Myst* follow-up, *Riven*. Yet even if you missed another one of our favorite 1997 films, *Sick: The Life and Death of Bob Flanagan, Supermasochist*, you must know there is no pleasure without pain. And on our reviewers' worst-of lists can be found some real doozies. Still, while pondering *The Island of Dr. Moreau*, you have to wonder: Could today's stinker be tomorrow's guilty pleasure?

Boogie Nights

1 Paul Thomas Anderson's delirious porn-world epic is the most sheerly pleasurable movie I saw all year, and what makes it such a kicky and resonant experience is that its very subject is pleasure. Tracing the rise and fall of Dirk Diggler, a triple-X superstar who rides the waves of post-counterculture hedonism until he can't stand up anymore, Anderson roots his movie in a definitive re-creation of the funky, bedazzled, cocaine-and-disco '70s, an era that is only just beginning to enter the realm of pop mythology because it now seems like the last moment in American life when people simply did what they wanted. Anderson embodies that ecstatic, shoot-the-works spirit in the gleeful freedom of his filmmaking. You feel, at every moment, that he's in love with what he's showing you, whether it's Mark Wahlberg, as Dirk, flashing his beautiful gaze of macho innocence as he dreams of becoming a "big bright shining star"; the high comedy of on-set porn shoots that play like *Ed Wood* without clothes; the cocky desperation of Burt Reynolds' fleshpot auteur saying *"Sexy!"* in the back of a limo as he "directs" a gruesomely unerotic hardcore video; the ferocity of Heather Graham's Rollergirl removing her cheerleader mask to reveal the scary rage beneath; or—the year's most indelible scene—the thrill-happy dementia of Alfred Molina's motormouth addict merging himself with the chorus of "Sister Christian," a song that, in *Boogie Nights*, becomes a heavy metal requiem, a shrine to the eternal, unholy American quest for the next high.

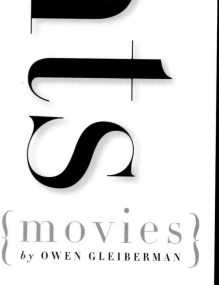

{ movies }
by OWEN GLEIBERMAN

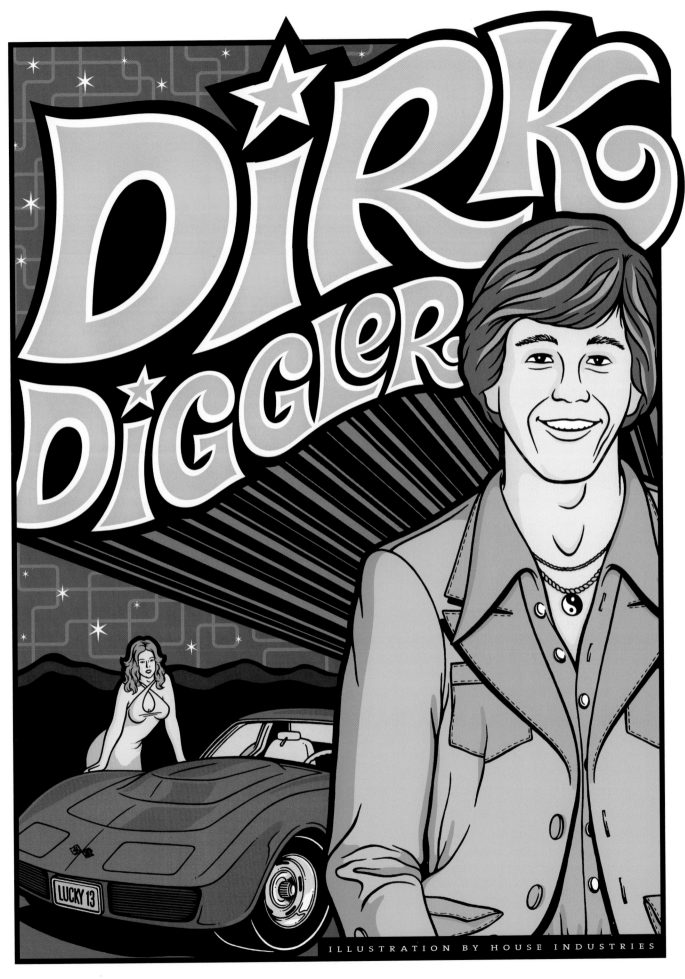

ILLUSTRATION BY HOUSE INDUSTRIES

DEATH BECOMES THEM: Tragedy strikes both *Hereafter* (with Sarah Polley, above center) and *Titanic* (with DiCaprio and Winslet, below)

2 THE SWEET HEREAFTER In this hypnotic modern fairy tale set in the snowy desolation of British Columbia, writer-director Atom Egoyan proves a master of rapturous emotional storytelling. The puzzle-obsessed gamesmanship of his previous work hasn't gone away, though. It's there in the teasing, lapidary brilliance with which he structures this adaptation of Russell Banks' novel about the aftermath of a fatal school-bus accident. Egoyan, like a postmodern Hitchcock, reveals the details of the disaster only gradually, until it seems to have emerged from a disturbance in the universe. *The Sweet Hereafter* is a hymn to parental bereavement, yet you haven't fully taken in the movie if you think it's simply about the calamity of lost children, the impotent love with which questing attorney Ian Holm regards his homeless druggie daughter, or the incestuous relationship between a local teenager and her father. A work of spellbinding mysticism, *The Sweet Hereafter* is about the elusive connection between all those things— about a world in which darkness spreads invisibly, only to be checked by an equally ineffable voice of light.

3 TITANIC A miraculous entertainment that proves the magic of Hollywood is far from gone. In his haunting disaster epic, writer-director James Cameron orchestrates the kind of lush, old-style, grander-than-life spectacle that you thought no one made any-more. Leonardo DiCaprio and Kate Winslet bring a cunning and playful sensuality to their opposite-sides-of-the-tracks love story, and the film invites us to revel in everything about their relationship that might, in the wrong hands, have devolved into winsome cliché. Where *Titanic* becomes a genuinely great movie—indeed, a film unlike any other—is in its mesmerizing final hour, where Cameron stages the sinking of the *Titanic* with an awe-inspiring realism unimaginable before the era of contemporary special effects. He puts us right on board that ship, creating a poeticized vision of 20th-century doom—clear-eyed, terrifying, impossibly romantic.

4 L.A. CONFIDENTIAL The screen just about glows with corruption, with the sleazy vitality of dirty deeds. The first crime thriller in more than two decades that truly earns comparison with *Chinatown*, Curtis Hanson's smoldering adaptation of James Ellroy's underbelly-of-Los Angeles-in-the-'50s novel has a plot as twisty and treacherous as a nest of vipers. The cast is led by three extraordinary actors: Guy Pearce, his mind as vivid as some people's fists, as a noble cop who has to learn to get down in the muck; Russell Crowe, his hunky glower finally coming into star focus, as a brutal cop who has to raise himself out of it; and Kevin Spacey, that genie of acerbic nonchalance, who, as a cynical celebrity officer, finds a grace note of tragedy within the tabloid effervescence.

5 THE APOSTLE Robert Duvall plays Sonny, a Pentecostal minister who's a family man, a skirt-chasing sinner, a moonstruck narcissist, and also one of the most profoundly religious characters ever put on a movie screen. Duvall, who wrote, directed, and financed *The Apostle*, makes you feel, with an almost physical force, the cleansing intensity of Sonny's faith, the way it inflames the air around him. Sonny is a transcendent preacher, in part because he revels in his own power nearly as much as he does in God's. The movie is about the fall and redemption of a good but deeply flawed man, and Duvall, in the greatest performance of the year (indeed, the performance of his life), makes that journey feel as hot as blood, as tender as tears.

6 THE WINGS OF THE DOVE At last, a literary period piece that's about something more than the conflict between aristocratic repression and sensual liberation. Director Iain Softley finds the sublime heart of Henry James' 1902 novel about a clandestine couple (Helena Bonham Carter and Linus Roache) in turn-of-the-century London who have already figured out the sensual-liberation part. The trouble is, they don't have any money, so they repress their moral judgment to go through with a disquieting plan—the seduction of a dying heiress (Alison Elliott) who, they hope, will leave them her fortune.

Dazzlingly photographed and thrillingly acted, especially by Bonham Carter, who shows a new complexity and womanly radiance, *The Wings of the Dove* comes as close as anyone has to getting James, in all his lyrical ripeness, on screen.

7 WAITING FOR GUFFMAN Comedy should lift the soul, and my soul still hasn't come down from seeing *Waiting for Guffman*, the most exquisite rib-tickler in years. Directed and cowritten by its star, Christopher Guest, who filmed it in the same mockumentary style as *This Is Spiñal Tap* (this one, though, is even funnier), it follows the hapless residents of Blaine, Mo., as they write, squabble over, and finally

WINGS OF DESIRE: Elliott, Alex Jennings, and Bonham Carter lift *Dove*

perform, in their very own high school gymnasium, an all-singing, all-dancing, all-excruciating musical homage to their beloved hometown. If there were any justice, Guest's performance as Corky St. Clair, the town's flaming theatrical "genius" ("I hate you, and I hate your *ass face!*"), would be on its way to an Oscar nomination.

8 SICK: THE LIFE AND DEATH OF BOB FLANAGAN, SUPERMASOCHIST Bob Flanagan was a self-lacerating performance artist who suffered from cystic fibrosis. He martyred his flesh in order to master his pain. (He also did it because it turned him on.) In Kirby Dick's brilliant, unsettling documentary, Flanagan emerges as one of the richest, strangest, most heroic film presences of 1997, a witty alchemist of psychosexual torment who turned his own body into a hideous work of art. *Sick* proved too extreme to win many viewers, but it's an extraordinary vérité parable, a portrait of how far one man will go to spit at the forces that spawned him.

9 DONNIE BRASCO New York Italian mobsters in the mid-1970s. An aging hitman. A young FBI agent who goes undercover and befriends him. Sound like things you've seen before? You have. But in the hands of Paul Attanasio, who may be the last classi-

HURTS SO GOOD: Depp's Brasco (above) learns to play by Mob rules; *Sick*'s Flanagan (below, with lover Sheree Rose) blurs pleasure and pain

cal screenwriter in Hollywood (he must feel like an undercover agent himself), *Donnie Brasco* fashions its familiar elements into a nimble and intricate true-life tale of crime, deception, and torn loyalty. For the first time, Johnny Depp, who plays the agent, succeeds in making his cool-hand reserve zing in a normal-guy role, and Al Pacino, as the gangster who doesn't realize he's run out of time, is surprisingly moving. He's the wiseguy as Willy Loman.

10 IN THE COMPANY OF MEN

A movie that's this heady a conversation piece runs the risk of seeming little *more* than a conversation piece. But Neil LaBute's joyously savage drama of corporate misanthropy only pretends not to have a soul. Its riveting tale of two glib white-collar drones who decide to woo, then dump, a beautiful, deaf assistant is really a study in how far some men will go to downsize their emotions in order to preserve their distance from each other. Aaron Eckhart's performance is mean, funny, and layered. Look closely, and you'll see that the trick of the movie is that he really *does* fall in love with his deaf victim. The horror of the movie is that even that's not enough to make him care.

Critical Mass

A SAMPLING OF 50 NOTABLE MOVIES FROM 1997—HITS, FLOPS, CRITICS' FAVES, AND A FEW SLEEPERS—AS GRADED BY AUDIENCES AND SELECTED REVIEWERS

	CINEMASCORE Audiences across the U.S.	ROGER EBERT Siskel & Ebert	GENE SISKEL Siskel & Ebert	JAMI BERNARD Knight-Ridder Syndicate	CARRIE RICKEY Knight-Ridder Syndicate	MIKE CLARK USA Today	ENTERTAINMENT WEEKLY	CRITICS' AVERAGE
THE SWEET HEREAFTER	—	A	A–	A	A	A–	A	A
TITANIC	—	A	B+	A–	—	A	A	A–
BOOGIE NIGHTS	C	A	B+	A	B	A+	A	A–
L.A. CONFIDENTIAL	A–	A–	B+	A	B+	A–	A	A–
IN THE COMPANY OF MEN	—	A	B+	B+	—	B	A	A–
« FACE/OFF	B+	B	B+	A+	B–	B	A	B+
IN & OUT	B	B	B+	A–	A–	B–	A–	B+
DONNIE BRASCO	B+	B+	B	B+	B+	B+	A–	B+
THE WINGS OF THE DOVE	—	B+	B	B	A–	C+	A	B+
THE APOSTLE	—	A–	B	B	—	B	A–	B+
« HERCULES	A	B	C+	A–	B	A–	A–	B+
THE FULL MONTY	A–	B	A–	B+	B	B+	B	B+
CONTACT	A–	B+	B	B–	A–	B–	B+	B
WELCOME TO SARAJEVO	—	C	B+	B+	—	B	A–	B
MEN IN BLACK	B+	B–	B+	B+	B+	B+	C+	B
CHASING AMY	—	A–	B	B–	B	B–	B+	B
SCREAM 2	—	B–	B	B+	B	B–	A–	B
AIR FORCE ONE	A	C+	B	B+	C+	B	A	B
ABSOLUTE POWER	B+	A	C+	A	B–	C	C	B
« THE GAME	B–	B+	C+	B+	C+	B+	B+	B
STARSHIP TROOPERS	C+	C–	B	B+	C+	A	B+	B
ANASTASIA	A–	B+	B–	B–	B	B	B–	B
CONSPIRACY THEORY	B+	C+	B–	A	B–	B	C+	B
BREAKDOWN	B	B–	C+	C	B	B+	A–	B
GROSSE POINTE BLANK	B	D+	C+	B+	B+	B	A–	B
AUSTIN POWERS: INTERNATIONAL MAN OF MYSTERY	B–	B–	B	C+	B–	A–	B	B–
THE DEVIL'S OWN	B–	C+	B+	C+	C+	B–	B+	B–
JOHN GRISHAM'S THE RAINMAKER	A–	B	B	B	B	B–	C	B–
THE FIFTH ELEMENT	B	B–	B+	A–	C+	C	B–	B–
ANACONDA	B–	B+	B	B	C–	B	B–	B–
« SOUL FOOD	A+	B+	B–	C+	B	C+	B–	B–
G.I. JANE	A–	B	B–	B–	B	C	B–	B–
AMISTAD	—	B	B+	B	B	C	C	B–
THE LOST WORLD	B+	C	B–	B	B–	B–	B	B–
THE PEACEMAKER	B+	C	B+	B+	C+	B–	C+	B–
« COP LAND	B–	C	B+	C	B	B	B–	B–
THE DEVIL'S ADVOCATE	B	C+	B	C+	C+	B–	B	B–
MY BEST FRIEND'S WEDDING	A–	B–	B	B+	C	C–	C+	B–
MIDNIGHT IN THE GARDEN OF GOOD AND EVIL	C+	C	B+	B	B	D+	C+	B–
ALIEN RESURRECTION	B–	C–	C–	C+	B–	B–	B–	C+
LOST HIGHWAY	—	C–	C	C	—	B–	B–	C+
DANTE'S PEAK	A–	C	C+	C	C	C+	C+	C+
BATMAN & ROBIN	C+	C	C	C	—	C+	C+	C
CON AIR	B+	B	B–	D	C	C	C	C
KISS THE GIRLS	B+	B+	C	D	C	C	C	C
VOLCANO	B+	D+	C+	B	C–	D	B–	C
SPEED 2: CRUISE CONTROL	B–	B	B	C	D+	D	D+	C
« I KNOW WHAT YOU DID LAST SUMMER	B–	D	F	B–	—	C+	B–	C–
THE SAINT	B+	C–	C+	B–	C	D+	F	C–
FLUBBER	B+	F	C	D	C+	D–	B–	D+

A Second Opinion {movies}

1. L.A. CONFIDENTIAL So *this* is what happens when everything comes together—subject matter and style, plot and script, performance and cinematography, and the confidence of director Curtis Hanson to take on James Ellroy's complicated, pungent novel about 1950s Hollywood lowlife. You get an award-worthy 1990s Hollywood movie—a model of flawless cinematic storytelling.

2. TITANIC When people talk about the magic of the movies, they mean this— James Cameron's huge, impeccably produced epic in which every single shot is dedicated to telling a big story in a way that doesn't just fill our eyes with grandeur but also stirs our souls with awe.

3. IN THE COMPANY OF MEN Two young salarymen hatch a plan to humiliate a woman, simple as that. But in this stunning fable (beautifully written and acted, economically made), first-time writer-director Neil LaBute taps into a wellspring of rage, misogyny, and all-purpose misanthropy so hot the work singes our nerves.

4. ULEE'S GOLD No camera tricks, no special effects, no pretty boys angling to be the Next Big Thing. Victor Nuñez's graceful, soft-spoken story about an aging Florida beekeeper is old-fashioned storytelling at its most assured. It's also a chance for Peter Fonda (an ex–Next Big Thing) to do his best work in decades.

5. FACE/OFF John Woo's daredevil filmmaking—old news for fans of his Hong Kong movies—is a dazzling discovery for everyone else: It weaves haunting set pieces of choreographed violence, unusually nuanced characters, and joyful performances from John Travolta and Nicolas Cage into an intensely satisfying experience.

TO BEE OR NOT TO BEE: *Ulee*'s Fonda is pure gold

6. THE SWEET HEREAFTER Atom Egoyan's interpretation of Russell Banks' fine novel about tragedy (children in a small Canadian town drown when their school bus sinks), grief, and the ways folks make sense of the senseless is as crystalline-pure as cold northern air.

7. IN & OUT A sophisticated mainstream American comedy about modern, untortured homosexuality? That turns minority gay sensibility into a majority virtue? That makes you laugh out loud? Well, *yes*. This gem from writer Paul Rudnick and director Frank Oz proves that a comedy about homosexuals doesn't need to be loud to be proud.

8. PONETTE A child's-eye view of heartbreak in a drama about the death of a parent that's nearly unbearable in its intensity—yet absolutely gripping. In guiding the extraordinary performance of Victoire Thivisol (then 4 years old), French director Jacques Doillon is rewarded with honest vignettes of childhood at its most vulnerable.

9. EVE'S BAYOU The ghost of Tennessee Williams hovers over Kasi Lemmons' moss-draped story of sisters and their daddy in a Louisiana backwater. But the first-time writer-director creates a dreamy style entirely her own in this fluid, feminine, African-American, Southern gothic yarn—one that covers a tremendous amount of emotional territory with the lightest of steps.

10. THE APOSTLE Robert Duvall inhabits the soul of a flawed Christian who is also a great evangelist. He propels the drama (as producer, director, and writer) with the force of his own passion. And he blazes on screen in a hell-for-leather performance. Somebody say *Amen.* —*Lisa Schwarzbaum*

1. THE SAINT It sounded like a fun idea: Val Kilmer as a globe-trotting espionage bucko who's a master of disguise. Unfortunately, the movie never gets around to showing you how he changes into his disguises, *why* he changes into his disguises, or what it is, exactly, that he's doing. An effusion of plot holes so dense it seems to be unfolding in another dimension, *The Saint* is the apotheosis of the new incoherence. Not that Val Kilmer minds. Vamping madly beneath his wigs, as if in homage to the worst performances of Marlon Brando, he's like a new kind of drag king: a male male impersonator.

2. IRMA VEP Why don't French films matter anymore? Quite simply, because most of them suck. This was easily 1997's worst, an unbearably turgid, "structuralist" *Day for Night* that wowed some of the more gullible members of the fashion-victim set because it played as a compendium of Hong Kong chic, comic-book chic, dominatrix chic, and how-disaffected-are-we? chic. The movie is so disaffected it barely exists.

3. A LIFE LESS ORDINARY It was inevitable, perhaps, that the wild-boy Scottish creators of *Trainspotting* would come to America. What was less predictable is that they would do so to make a raucous yet "sweet" fable about an heiress, the Marxist janitor who kidnaps her, a pair of gun-toting angels, and, in a scene that makes you want to outlaw karaoke bars, Cameron Diaz and

FRENCH TOAST: *Irma Vep*'s laid-back Maggie Cheung

5 WORST

Ewan McGregor singing along with Bobby Darin's "Beyond the Sea." Back to Scotland, boys; may the weather clear your heads.

4. THE DESIGNATED MOURNER The playwright Wallace Shawn was a good writer until he started hectoring us about the demise of Western Civilization. In this egregiously overcooked diatribe, Mike Nichols stars as Shawn's mouthpiece, a jaded intellectual who feels so guilty about not reading books anymore that he proceeds to excoriate the rest of us for not reading books anymore. Nichols' performance, a singular feat of emphatic whining, makes you understand the high suicide rate among therapists.

5. SPEED 2: CRUISE CONTROL This time, a giant ocean liner stays afloat—it's the movie that sinks. How could an action wizard like Jan De Bont have agreed to direct a sequel to *Speed* that's set entirely aboard a cruise ship? You can't *do* speed on a cruise ship. Why? *Cruise ships aren't fast.* But you can certainly submerge the careers of Sandra Bullock and Jason Patric. —*OG*

TOP HITS

HOLLYWOOD REVELED IN RECYCLING in 1997, hauling in cash from old-style horror (*Scream 2*), made-to-profit sequels (*The Lost World*), and rereleased favorites (*Star Wars*). Will Smith grabbed the No. 1 spot for the second year with his *Men in Black*; the cheery action flick benefited from the delayed launch of *Titanic*, which busted box office records within a mere two weeks of its December release. —*Daniel Fierman*

Rank	Film / Studio / Star	Gross
1.	MEN IN BLACK *Columbia*, Will Smith	$250.1
2.	THE LOST WORLD: JURASSIC PARK *Universal*, Jeff Goldblum	$229.1
3.	LIAR LIAR *Universal*, Jim Carrey	$181.4
4.	AIR FORCE ONE *Columbia*, Harrison Ford	$171.5
5.	TITANIC *Paramount*, Kate Winslet	$157.5
6.	STAR WARS: SPECIAL EDITION *Fox*, Mark Hamill	$138.2
7.	MY BEST FRIEND'S WEDDING *TriStar*, Julia Roberts	$126.8
8.	FACE/OFF *Paramount*, John Travolta	$112.3
9.	BATMAN & ROBIN *Warner Bros.*, George Clooney	$107.3
10.	GEORGE OF THE JUNGLE *Walt Disney*, Brendan Fraser	$105.3
11.	CON AIR *Touchstone*, Nicolas Cage	$100.9
12.	CONTACT *Warner Bros.*, Jodie Foster	$100.8
13.	HERCULES *Walt Disney*, Animated	$99.1
14.	TOMORROW NEVER DIES *MGM/UA*, Pierce Brosnan	$92.4
15.	SCREAM 2 *Dimension*, Neve Campbell	$85.5
16.	FLUBBER *Walt Disney*, Robin Williams	$83.1
17.	CONSPIRACY THEORY *Warner Bros.*, Mel Gibson	$75.9
18.	I KNOW WHAT YOU DID LAST SUMMER *Columbia*, Jennifer Love Hewitt	$69.7
19.	THE EMPIRE STRIKES BACK: SPECIAL EDITION *Fox*, Mark Hamill	$67.6
20.	DANTE'S PEAK *Universal*, Pierce Brosnan	$67.1
21.	ANACONDA *Columbia*, Jennifer Lopez	$65.6
22.	THE FIFTH ELEMENT *Columbia*, Bruce Willis	$63.5
23.	IN & OUT *Paramount*, Kevin Kline	$63.4
24.	THE SAINT *Paramount*, Val Kilmer	$61.4
25.	JUNGLE2JUNGLE *Walt Disney*, Tim Allen	$59.9

Note: Figures are 1997 box office grosses, in millions; source: Exhibitor Relations Co. Inc.

King *of the* Hill

1

{television} *by* KEN TUCKER

(Fox) It was a good year for new cartoons, but I'll take *King of the Hill*'s bracing openheartedness over *South Park*'s clever but monotonous heartlessness any time. TV's most original, complicated new character was Hank Hill—middle-class Texan, political conservative, social libertarian, Willie Nelson fan—who exploded every white-guy small-screen stereotype in place since Archie Bunker. Best supporting players: son Bobby, TV's most lovable new child star, and Hank's sweetly shrewd wife, Peggy (voiced by Kathy Najimy, doing a great job with better lines than she gets on *Veronica's Closet*). Series creators Mike Judge and Greg Daniels use the cartoon format to commit creative murder: No live-action show would have gotten away with the constipation episode (in which Hank's colon serves as a window to his soul) or a plot about the use of crack as fish bait. Well, *ER* might have tried the colon-soul one, but it would have been really *grrr-ooosss*.

2 EVERYBODY LOVES RAYMOND *(CBS)* Not only did this superlatively old-fashioned sitcom become a solid success (by moving to Mondays), it also became a better show. I hate to compliment a guy for deftness when his funniness depends on seeming awkward, but really, Ray Romano is doing more with a deadpan and a drone than many other TV actors do with years of theater-honed technique. This is the only family show right now that gets as much of its humor from silence (the exquisite slow burns that Romano, Patricia Heaton, and Brad Garrett each deploy to convey their individual comic agonies) as from punchlines. A classic in the making.

3 BUFFY THE VAMPIRE SLAYER *(The WB)* By contrast, there's nothing classic about *Buffy*—its pleasure derives from the way it so giddily leeches off the pop culture of the moment. Tapping into the market for teen horror that he himself helped create, writer-producer Joss Whedon mingled post-*Clueless* slang with *Scream*-like sangfroid to come up with one groovy hour, week after week. Years from now (heck, probably *one* year from now), its in-jokes and silly scares will seem as stilted and rococo as Jack Kerouac's hipster lingo—or *Clueless*—does now.

4 OZ *(HBO)* One of the only artists working in pop culture in 1997 who pushed the boundaries of his medium, writer-producer Tom Fontana is also the only person in the history of television to accomplish this in part with a really artistically shot defecation/torture scene. This harrowing look into prison life featured extraordinary acting combined with stories that frequently managed to be horrific, hilarious, and bone-shakingly moving all in the same episode. Describing an edition of *Oz* to a non–HBO subscriber frequently gave new usefulness to Jack Paar's old catchphrase "I kid you not."

5 THE SIMPSONS *(Fox)* "I say there are some things we don't want to know—*important* things!" Thus spake Ned Flanders, deeply spiritual nitwit, once again embodying *The Simpsons'* perennial target: all-American dim-bulbedness. Television's most gleeful satire featured an especially strong Halloween episode in 1997, and Smithers' tortured crush on Mr. Burns took on an intensity of pre-out *Ellen* proportions. Some of its best plots managed to make little Lisa's existence more complicated and poignant; unlike everyone else on the show, she *wants* to know all the important things in life.

6 THE X-FILES *(Fox)* I'm hearing complaints from fans about how the "mythology" episodes have become glacially paced, niggling in the amount

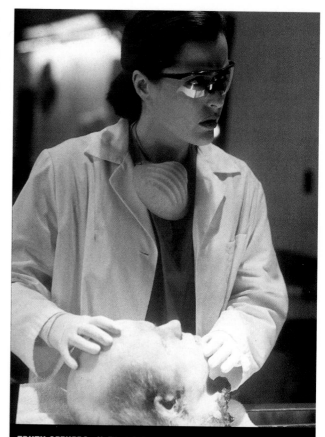

TRUTH SEEKERS: *X-Files'* Gillian Anderson (above); *Law's* Waterston, Carey Lowell, Jerry Orbach, Benjamin Bratt (below, from left)

of new info dispensed. But as the series proceeds, I realize that I (and, dare I presume, creator Chris Carter?) have always been in it for the richness of the emotional, not the science-fictional, payoffs. Which is to say, Scully's cancer remission was handled with a lovely restraint that has led to a renewed dramatic energy: *The X-Files* has become, in an almost classical sense, a romantic quest. The "monster" episodes (such as the lyrical Frankenstein/Cher/Jerry Springer entry) now carry more human resonance, as do the dry, sarcastic comments Mulder and Scully make to each other to stave off the boredom of work and the disaster of an affair.

7 LAW & ORDER *(NBC)* The equivalent of reading a good police procedural and a solid courtroom thriller every week—an unbeatable prime-time accomplishment. Special credit goes to Sam Waterston for being so willing to play Assistant DA Jack McCoy as a distracted, sad, grumpy, and work-obsessed jerk.

8 ER *(NBC)* The most popular drama on television refuses to become complacent. No, I didn't like the live episode either, but that one aside, *ER*'s undiminished energy is impressive, its layered subplots engrossing. More kudos to an actor opting to play unsympathetic: I never thought I'd be caught up in Anthony Edwards' Mark Greene character until he turned petulant and snarky.

9 NEWSRADIO *(NBC)* Television's most intricately clever sitcom seemed, if anything, even more shrewd in 1997, as creator Paul Simms and his writers used the show's low network visibility to their advantage, moving characters around like chess pieces (Let's fire Andy Dick's Matthew! Let's demote Dave Foley's character! Khandi Alexander wants to leave? We'll kiss her off in style!). The result is something sitcoms rarely prove to be: surprising.

10 DHARMA & GREG *(ABC)* Unnoted by critic-fans intent on celebrating her bodaciousness is Jenna Elfman's ability to do what so many women playing ditsy girls have failed at: She has proved to possess a real range of emotions within the limits of that ditsy-girl comic creation. Thomas Gibson is one of the best straight men TV has seen in years, and if the hippie jokes for Dharma's parents are getting as thin as Alan Rachins' ponytail, the funniness of Susan Sullivan's soul-dead grande dame just keeps getting deeper.

{television}
A Second Opinion

LIFE SUPPORT: Andre Braugher (right) with Vincent D'Onofrio

1. **HOMICIDE: LIFE ON THE STREET** *(NBC)* and OZ *(HBO)* TV's finest writer, Tom Fontana, explores both sides of the law in these groundbreaking series. *Homicide* hit a new high with an epic investigation of a murder in a wealthy African-American family. And freed from network censors, the grim prison drama *Oz* demolished almost every last TV taboo, without ever seeming exploitative.

2. **EVERYBODY LOVES RAYMOND** *(CBS)* Ray Romano's family sitcom delved deep into suburban dysfunction. No sitcom enjoyed a better batting average: Every episode has been a home run.

3. **NEWSRADIO** *(NBC)* The sly office satire took a surreal turn in 1997, with the entire ensemble following in superspaz Andy Dick's slapstick footsteps. Even with Khandi

Alexander's exit, the cast continue to be a nearly peerless comedy troupe.

4. **FRASIER** *(NBC)* After more than 100 half hours, the new episodes of Kelsey Grammer's farce still stand proudly next to its reruns. Wish I could say the same for *Seinfeld*.

5. **ELLEN** *(ABC)* The "coming out" episode was a pop-culture miracle: a media circus that lived up to its hype. Ever since then, Ellen DeGeneres' sitcom has radiated with the sheer joy of creative freedom.

6. **BUFFY THE VAMPIRE SLAYER** *(The WB)* The genius of this teen screamer is its treatment of supernatural combat as just another high school nightmare. Sarah Michelle Gellar balances dating dilemmas with demon destruction.

7. **THE CHRIS ROCK SHOW** *(HBO)* Rock this: The bitingly brilliant stand-up packs more attitude into his half-hour-a-week talk show than Dave, Jay, Conan, and Keenen do in 20 hours *combined*.

8. **THE GREGORY HINES SHOW** *(CBS)* Who knew the hoofer would step so smoothly into TV dad-dom? The jokes can be predictable, but costars Brandon Hammond, Wendell Pierce, and Bill Cobbs ground them in true familial affection.

9. **GEORGE & LEO** *(CBS)* God-among-funnymen Bob Newhart is at his best among a cast of crazies, and his new series has plenty: Judd Hirsch, Jason Bateman, and the deliciously dry Darryl Theirse as Bob's underpaid employee.

10. **THE DAILY SHOW** *(Comedy Central)* This mock newscast's anchor, Craig Kilborn, reigns as TV's supreme smartass—and the logical heir to *SNL*'s Norm Macdonald, who seems increasingly uninterested in doing "Weekend Update." —*Bruce Fretts*

UNHIP TO BE *SQUARE*: This sitcom *Union* should be dissolved

3. HITZ *(UPN)* Like UFOs, Andrew Dice Clay is an inexplicable phenomenon. Unable to read a line so the words cohere as a sentence, he still manages to get work as a professional misogynist. The fact that new UPN president Dean Valentine yanked the bad-but-harmless *Head Over Heels* and left this insidiousness on only adds to the mystery.

4. UNHAPPILY EVER AFTER *(The WB)* Filling the Sunday-night vulgarity void left by *Married...With Children*, this stupidly written sitcom exists primarily to force the actually not-bad actress Nikki Cox to prance around in tiny dresses and spike heels, amid catcalls from the audience. Cruel, pandering, creepy; please cancel so I can stop watching every week.

5. ARLI$$ *(HBO)* A sentimental (un-)favorite, with added bitterness in 1997: Robert Wuhl's mirthless sports rip-off of *The Larry Sanders Show* was a reminder that we endured without any new *Larry*s since February. —*Ken Tucker*

1. PAULY *(Fox)* It was so bad, the howling studio audience could not recognize the illiterate punchlines, and therefore just howled all the time. It was so bad, even the usually shameless Pauly Shore looked abashed.

2. UNION SQUARE *(NBC)* The answer to the question, What would happen if they put a sitcom on between *Friends* and *Seinfeld* and nobody cared?

TOP HITS

CALL IT AN OMINOUS SEIN OF THE TIMES. In the 1996–97 season, any sitcom following NBC's *Seinfeld* on Thursday instantly became Must See TV. Newcomers *Suddenly Susan* and *Fired Up*, plus sophomore effort *The Naked Truth*, all filled that slot at some point— and saw ratings soar. At ABC, there was cause for both elation (*The Drew Carey Show* went from 48th to 18th) and concern (*Home Improvement* slipped from 5th to 8th, while *Grace Under Fire* slipped from 14th to 49th). And at CBS, *60 Minutes* dropped out of the top 10 for the first time in 20 years, while *Touched by an Angel* soared from 23rd to 10th. As for 11-year-old Fox, execs uncorked champagne when *The X-Files* moved into the top 15. —*Shawna Malcom*

1. ER *NBC*				**30.8**
2. Seinfeld *NBC*	30.6	14. CBS Sunday Movie		17.5
3. Friends *NBC*	24.9	15. NBC Sunday Night Movie		17.5
4. Suddenly Susan *NBC*	24.6	16. NYPD Blue *ABC*		17.4
5. The Naked Truth *NBC*	24.5	17. Spin City *ABC*		17.3
6. Fired Up *NBC*	23.5	18. The Drew Carey Show *ABC*		17.0
7. NFL Monday Night Football *ABC*	22.7	19. 3rd Rock From the Sun *NBC*		17.0
8. Home Improvement *ABC*	21.7	20. Walker, Texas Ranger *CBS*		17.0
9. The Single Guy *NBC*	20.9	21. Soul Man *ABC*		16.7
10. Touched by an Angel *CBS*	20.3	22. Frasier *NBC*		16.6
11. 60 Minutes *CBS*	18.8	23. PrimeTime Live *ABC*		16.1
12. 20/20 *ABC*	18.3	24. Cosby *CBS*		16.0
13. The X-Files *Fox*	18.3	25. Mad About You *NBC*		15.7

Note: Figures are in millions of viewers

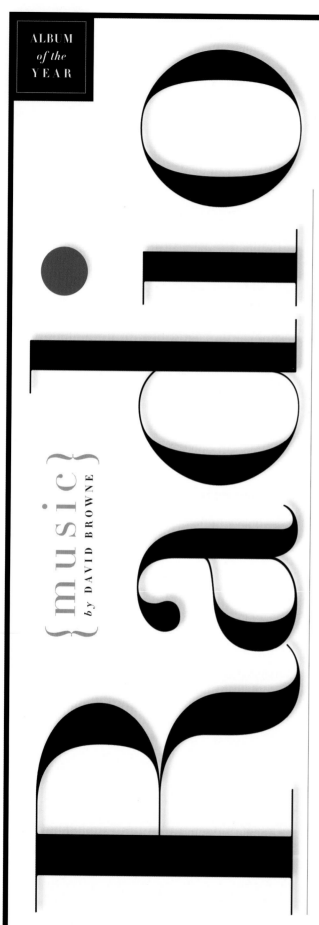

{music}
by DAVID BROWNE

01

Contemplating the world around him through squinty eyes, Thom Yorke, lead singer and song-writer of Radiohead, would rather tune himself out. In his songs, all he sees are cynical politicians and excessively regimented lifestyles, and he'd prefer to wait for aliens to scoop him up for an intergalactic ride. Weary of the draining intensity of modern life, Yorke is in search of "no alarms and no surprises," as he sings in one of his cryptic lyrics, and he's looking for a higher ground, a fresh start. On Radiohead's most ambitious album, he's found it. When we first heard from them some four years ago, Radiohead were egregious grunge clones—and from England at that. Three albums later, they've come into their own on this subtly resplendent opus.

HEAD

Wafting, swelling, and subsiding in billowy bursts, the songs aren't rock or electronica, but a celestial place somewhere in between. As each song segues gracefully into the next, *OK Computer* becomes a cohesive album—remember those?—with Yorke's frail sigh, which glides to a falsetto before inevitably crashing down, providing the glue. No other piece of music in 1997 so eloquently captured fin de siècle wariness, the gnawing sense that a new, scary, and potentially enlightening world may be only two years away. Until the UFOs arrive, the sullen grandeur of *OK Computer* will have to suffice for Yorke, and for the rest of us, too.

MAKING *AUTUMN SWEETER:* Hushed intensity from Yo La Tengo

2 DIG YOUR OWN HOLE The Chemical Brothers *(Astralwerks/Caroline, album)* On stage, Tom Rowlands and Ed Simons are the first techno act to make like rock stars: Lurching their computers back and forth, they look like Butt-head and Garth partying in a cybercafé. And their kinetic, incessantly inventive second album makes like rock too. Capturing the rave-new-world intensity of their concerts, *Dig Your Own Hole* is a series of relentless, playful romps that merge the futuristic grind and caffeinated break beats of techno with the walloping power of rock (and the occasional human voice, like that of Oasis' Noel Gallagher). No, 1997 didn't turn out to be the year in which electronica conquered the charts, but albums like

Dig Your Own Hole accomplished something more important than breaking sales records: They challenged accepted notions of song structures and dynamics while tapping into the same creativity and energy that once epitomized rock.

3 "YOUR WOMAN" White Town *(Chrysalis/ EMI, single)* Is it the sexual ambiguity of the lyrics? The alluring clip-clop of the beat? Or the forlorn quality of that voice, which sounds like a bereft lover calling ultra-long-distance? Whatever the reasons, what could have been a goofy dance-club novelty is instead a poignant dance-club romantic tragedy, courtesy of British one-man band Jyoti Mishra. Bonus points for

sneaking the phrase "your highbrow Marxist ways" onto Top 40 radio.

4 MIDDLE OF NOWHERE Hanson *(Mercury, album)* You've got a right to be sick of "MMMBop," but last summer's most refreshing musical water sprinkler is merely one of a dozen kicky treats on the major-label debut of these brothers from Tulsa. Christian milk imbibers who can sing, write, and play, they're no New Kids clones (that dubious honor goes to the Backstreet Boys) but rather a genuine oasis of pop soulfulness and melody. (Keep an eye, and ear, on Taylor.) From the start ("Thinking of You," which sprouts wings and flies) to its finish (the joyful teen grunge of "Man From Milwaukee [Garage Mix]"), *Middle of Nowhere* is the kind of pure, exhilarating pop no one seems to make anymore, and that's a shame. In an mmmbop they might be gone, but when the music's this infectious, who cares?

5 SUPA DUPA FLY Missy "Misdemeanor" Elliott *(EastWest, album)* What makes this former behind-the-scenes rap songwriter fly on her own isn't just her voice—a loose, smooth instrument that swoops from singing to rapping with fluid ease. It's her knack for a hook. Spotlighting the work of producer Timbaland, these odes to self-reliance, self-worth, feckless men, and playing stewardess tug at your ear with deft samples and beats; "Beep Me 911" even tips its wool hat to electronica. Elliott's inordinately tuneful, sensual hip-hop outclasses every other rap album in 1997 and puts Virginia Beach on the pop map. Besides, "vroom" never sounds so sexy as when it comes from Missy's mouth.

6 THE MAGNIFICENT SEVEN Okay, follow closely: Members of R.E.M., Screaming Trees, and Luna form Tuatara, an alt-rock supergroup—yes, it has come to this—and record *Breaking the Ethers* (Epic), an album of alluring country-and-Eastern instrumentals. Tuatara then backs Mark Eitzel on *West* (Warner Bros.), providing the hangdog singer-songwriter with his most bracing musical support to date. Then the whole caravan, under the rubric the Magnificent Seven, hits the road for a series of inspiring shows. For all the talk of the return of cocktail music, this pairing—Tuatara's

marimba-and-sax lounge noir and Eitzel's sulky, drink-saturated odes to self-loathing and wrenching excess—evokes the genre's spirit and its dimly lit bars better than, say, the soundtrack to *My Best Friend's Wedding.*

7 "AUTUMN SWEATER" Yo La Tengo *(Matador, single)* Romantic expectation, hesitation, disappointment, hope, and hopelessness, sung and played with the hushed intensity of a hymn. Last year's most moving indie-rock single and another peak for this New Jersey trio.

8 LETS GET KILLED David Holmes *(1500/A&M, album)* The trouble with all those soundscape, jungle, and drum-and-bass techno records flooding the market isn't content but atmosphere. So many of them feel antiseptic and rhythmically challenged—a bland revolution. Holmes, a Belfast DJ, solves that problem on this sublimely weird and funky debut. Holmes is terrific at concocting boingy beats and shuffles that stick to your ribs, but he doesn't stop there. He sprinkles the tracks with sonic grime, like Latin percussion and snippets of actual street-crazy conversations taped on the streets of New York. (Imagine a Tarantino soundtrack sans a movie.) Holmes' electronica crawls out of the recording studio and into the street—and springs to life in the process.

9 "HOW BIZARRE" OMC *(Huh!/Mercury, single)* and "DREAM" Forest for the Trees *(DreamWorks, single)* (tie) Nothing is simple anymore, least of all pop—in the post-Beck universe, all musical hell has broken loose. These two singles, by "bands" that are in fact one-man outfits, are last year's most vibrant examples of the new Cuisinart pop. Both share hip-hop beats and delectable female-chanted choruses, tossing in flamenco guitar and harmonica ("How Bizarre," New Zealander Pauly Fuemana's sly ode to a couple on the lam) or swirling sitars and bagpipes ("Dream," former Beck collaborator Carl Stephenson's hash-brownie reverie). Chaos never sounded so inviting.

TECH TONIC: The Chemical Brothers rock the rave new world

10 "WANNABE" and "SAY YOU'LL BE THERE" Spice Girls *(Virgin, singles)* Uncle.

PHOTOGRAPH BY DAVID BARRY

{music}
A Second Opinion

HOP ON *POP*: U2's Bono performs during the band's 1997 United States tour

1. POP U2 *(Island)* That's *Pop* as in "Pop Muzik," and *Pop* as in Father: This may be the first party record about the absence of God. But fans focused more on the techno sprinklings around the rim than the deus-shaped hole at the CD's center. So while it's weird calling a U2 album "criminally underrated," this one's rep may require years of rehabilitation. All in good time. "Gone" in particular is a great, rapturous funeral song for the ages; thank heaven no one thought to spoil it by hitching it to Di's wagon.

2. GUN SHY TRIGGER HAPPY Jen Trynin *(Squint/Warner Bros.)* The finest new rock slinger of the late '90s has a breakup song for every occasion. Chrissie Hynde has had plenty of pretend heirs, but Trynin—marrying cautious strains of ambivalence to cocky guitar pop—establishes a line of beautifully surly succession.

3. FRANK SINATRA WITH THE RED NORVO QUINTET, LIVE IN AUSTRALIA, 1959 Frank Sinatra *(Blue Note)* What a find: Old Bloodshot Eyes, riding his mid-1950s crest with a well-suited jazz combo, regarding one of the century's most considerable canons like a lovely bender.

4. OLE (THE PERSISTENCE OF MEMORY) Tonio K. *(Gadfly)* "Make it stop/Stop the clock forever," goes the opening chorus...and nope, it's not Dylan's celebrated meditation on mortality and time's ravages, but another great one in that subgenre from cult figure K., turning temporality into rock-of-ages stuff.

5. TIME OUT OF MIND Bob Dylan *(Columbia)* Dylan seems determined to sound as ghostly in the present tense as his hero Jimmie Rodgers does decades distant. These are blues heard through a glass darkly, the faint hope of heaven only occasionally casting light on last year's most impressively depressing long-form lament.

6. SONGS FROM THE CAPEMAN Paul Simon *(Warner Bros.)* In some ways this 13-song excerpt can't help but seem like a teaser for the 39-song Broadway show. But it's rewarding to hear Simon work out his heady themes in middlebrow character...and in soaring doo-wop and salsa.

7. OK COMPUTER Radiohead *(Capitol)* Sure, it's whiny. Sure, it's stunning. Karma police, promote this band!

8. WHATEVER AND EVER AMEN Ben Folds Five *(550 Music)* If any comer seems a smart bet to someday follow Simon onto Broadway, it's Folds, whose awesomely well-constructed, sober ballads are even better than his piano-pounding flights of bumblebee smart-aleckiness.

9. THE CHARITY OF NIGHT Bruce Cockburn *(Rykodisc)* Paint it black: This perennially cerebral Canadian's folk-noir cycle affectingly found humankind's best of times and worst under cover of darkness.

10. IN IT FOR THE MONEY Supergrass *(Capitol)* The perfect tonic for Oasis' mediocre bloat, Supergrass helped Brit pop earn back its good name by combining Supertramp with super-glam-rock. —*Chris Willman*

SAMADHI STOP THEM: Live may be the death of rock & roll

5 WORST

the sloppiest excuse for a superstar follow-up since Vanilla Ice's live album, by a young woman with a whole lotta voice and a whole little sense of what to do with it.

3. LIVE, SECRET SAMADHI (*Radioactive, album*) If this humorless, self-important twaddle is what rock has become, then maybe the genre really is dead after all.

4. WYCLEF JEAN, "WE TRYING TO STAY ALIVE" (*Columbia, single*) Say what you will about the Fugees, at least they record their own versions of oldies rather than resort to lazy sampling—or they did, that is, until this needless Bee Gees retread.

5. MATCHBOX 20, YOURSELF OR SOMEONE LIKE YOU (*Lava/Atlantic, album*) As if we need another reason to grouse about Counting Crows and Hootie: Their ascendance has given rise to a traffic jam of grating young dullards like this. Let's hope the woman who inspired the line "I want to take you for granted" (from the creepy hit "Push") is long gone. —*DB*

1. BOB CARLISLE, "BUTTERFLY KISSES" (*Diadem, single*) We're glad you're proud of your little girl, Bob, but did you have to set those emotions to soft-focus music that is more puke-inducing than morning sickness? And why did you then decide to overemote in a way that makes Michael Bolton sound understated by comparison?

2. LEANN RIMES, YOU LIGHT UP MY LIFE (*Curb, album*) The national anthem, "God Bless America," rote remakes of pop standards—a fine program for a state fair or a beauty-pageant contestant, but not something we want to hear from a major-league act. This is

TOP HITS

SPICEWORLD, INDEED. With four top 10 singles and two top 10 albums in '97, the girl group made everyone else seem like a wannabe. Should *more* girl power be required, though, the obvious choice would be No Doubt singer Gwen "alterna-Spice" Stefani, whose *Tragic Kingdom* took the No. 2 slot. As for the rest of the chart, rap and sap fared best: Earnest balladeers Jewel, LeAnn Rimes, Celine Dion, and the Wallflowers emoted their way to mega-sales, while Puffy Combs' *No Way Out* and the Notorious B.I.G.'s *Life After Death* (which was Puffy-produced) solidified Combs' clout. But the biggest story of '97? A slew of highly anticipated records that dropped faster than a Michael Jordan dunk: U2's career took a U-turn when *Pop* fizzled, while new albums from superstars like Aerosmith, Michael Jackson, and the Rolling Stones gathered more moss than moola. —*Rob Brunner*

TOP 12 ALBUMS	WEEKS ON CHART
1. SPICE, Spice Girls	48
2. TRAGIC KINGDOM, No Doubt	90
3. FALLING INTO YOU, Celine Dion	95
4. SOUNDTRACK, *Space Jam*	60
5. PIECES OF YOU, Jewel	99
6. BLUE, LeAnn Rimes	78
7. BRINGING DOWN THE HORSE, The Wallflowers	79
8. LIFE AFTER DEATH, Notorious B.I.G.	42
9. SECRETS, Toni Braxton	81
10. NO WAY OUT, Puff Daddy	24
11. RAZORBLADE SUITCASE, Bush	45
12. SOUNDTRACK, *Romeo & Juliet*	48

TOP 12 SINGLES	WEEKS ON CHART
1. CANDLE IN THE WIND 1997, Elton John	15
2. YOU WERE MEANT FOR ME, Jewel	60
3. I'LL BE MISSING YOU, Puff Daddy	32
4. UN-BREAK MY HEART, Toni Braxton	42
5. CAN'T NOBODY HOLD ME DOWN, Puff Daddy	28
6. I BELIEVE I CAN FLY, R. Kelly	34
7. DON'T LET GO (LOVE), En Vogue	35
8. RETURN OF THE MACK, Mark Morrison	40
9. HOW DO I LIVE, LeAnn Rimes	31
10. WANNABE, Spice Girls	23
11. QUIT PLAYING GAMES (WITH MY HEART), Backstreet Boys	30
12. MMMBOP, Hanson	22

1

CHARLES FRAZIER (ATLANTIC MONTHLY, $24)

It was a banner year for adventure stories of all kinds, but the remarkable thing about this one—an unabashedly literary first novel set during the Civil War—is that it throws the "coming home" part of adventure into sad, stark relief. A loose refashioning of the classic Odyssean myth, *Mountain* trails, in exquisitely researched detail, the treacherous 300-mile journey of a wounded Confederate deserter named Inman, a pilgrimage that leads back to Ada, the brilliant, cultured outsider whom he doesn't quite dare believe will become his wife. There is enough weapon clanging to satisfy all but the most bloodthirsty Civil War buffs, yet Frazier lavishes equal narrative weight on Ada's trials and ravaged psyche as she watches and waits, struggling to tend the farm of her dead father.

BOOK
of the
YEAR

Cold
MOUNTAIN

2 DAUGHTER OF THE QUEEN OF SHEBA Jacki Lyden *(Houghton Mifflin, $24)* It takes more than a *really crazy* mother to hoist a memoir above the herd. Not that this author's wasn't a doozy (Marie Antoinette was but one identity she adopted). But NPR senior correspondent Lyden doesn't just recount the heartbreakingly funny anecdotes of her mom's manic depression—she weaves them into a skein undergirding her own peripatetic life, with a graceful self-awareness.

3 INTO THIN AIR Jon Krakauer *(Villard, $24.95)* When *Outside* magazine sent Krakauer to report on a guided trip up Mount Everest in May 1996, he thought he'd be filing a piece about the summit's increasingly routine surmountability. By expedition's end, Everest had claimed six lives, and Krakauer had enough material for a book—one he would have given anything not to write. A horrifying, lucid survivor's account.

4 ALL OVER BUT THE SHOUTIN' Rick Bragg *(Pantheon, $25)* Nominally, this is the first-person story of how *New York Times* reporter Bragg went from his poor Alabama beginnings to a 1996 Pulitzer for feature writing. But it's really more of a poem disguised as a memoir, a gift from a son to his mother, plus a primer on good reporting. Bragg shows a flair for the unexpected metaphor, and compassion for his subjects.

5 APPETITE FOR LIFE: THE BIOGRAPHY OF JULIA CHILD Noël Riley Fitch *(Doubleday, $25.95)* Our beloved "lady of the ladle" threw open her life's chest of drawers—diaries, letters, falsies—to a scholar who'd previously chronicled erotic diarist Anaïs Nin, so be prepared for the naughty bits. But what total access mixed with zero interference from the Hearty One yields is a meaty, well-told life. *Bon appétit*, indeed.

6 UNDERWORLD Don DeLillo *(Scribner, $27.50)* After he lost to Frazier at 1997's National Book Awards, DeLillo walked around passing out his habitual note cards: "I don't want to talk about it." Even if he had, surely his powers of language were exhausted with this opus, which spans five decades and the entire Cold War. A dark, unflinching comedy about the psychic fallout of nuclear terror, it might not be DeLillo's Big Book, but it's a masterpiece nonetheless.

7 WHAT FALLS AWAY Mia Farrow *(Doubleday, $25; paperback Bantam, $7.50)* In one of the many priceless anecdotes in this grim fairy tale of an autobiography, French actor Charles Boyer tells the 10-year-old Farrow, "Your life will be a wonderful one, but difficult I think." And how! Pile the polio bout, the Sinatra and Previn marriages, the dozen or so kids, and *l'affaire* Woody onto her acting jobs, and it's amazing that the onetime *Peyton Place* waif can actually write. But she can—and well.

8 THE PERFECT STORM Sebastian Junger *(Norton, $23.95)* For once, it wasn't Stephen King behind the Most Nightmarish Passage of the Year. That honor goes to Junger, for his excruciating description of the sensation of drowning. Worse, this is nonfiction—the reconstruction of a fishing boat's engulfment by a freak convergence of three storms in 1991. Ferociously dramatic, vividly told—and totally tragic.

9 CROOKED LITTLE HEART Anne Lamott *(Pantheon, $24)* The bookish heroine of Lamott's 1983 novel *Rosie* has grown into a 13-year-old cheating tennis champ who, ruffled by the wayward ways of those around her, still mourns her long-dead dad. Set in the author's convivial, 12-step Northern California world, this beautiful, warbling sequel squeezes as much poetry as possible from a difficult adolescence.

10 HERE ON EARTH Alice Hoffman *(Putnam, $23.95)* For 20 years, Hoffman has spun stories that flit between serious literature and pop fiction, often overlaid with the gauze of magic. Her 12th novel is no exception: It starts with a woman visiting her hometown for a funeral, stirs in troubled characters, and ends with a darkly complicated brew of abuse, familial love, and female identity. Oprah, are you listening?

WRITER ON THE *STORM*: Junger spins a vivid—and tragic—tale

PHOTOGRAPH BY CHRISTOPHER KOLK

MORRIS CODE: The *Oval Office* author gets a vote of no–competence

5 WORST

(mincing gay sexual predator; manipulative Jewish banker), and a far sterner editing hand. One wonders whether this was written, or dictated on the run.

3. BOOK Whoopi Goldberg *(Rob Weisbach, $22)* You get a whiff of what you're in for (bromides, scatology) with this line of jacket copy: "This book doesn't suck." (Hey, don't put words in our mouths!) But for a rumored $6 million advance, is it so much to ask that *Book* do more than not suck?

4. BEHIND THE OVAL OFFICE Dick Morris *(Random House, $25.95)* Let this $2.5 million, 346-page wonk-fest plonk right down next to Marlon Brando's $5 million autobiography in the mirthless category of Books That Sent Random House Chief Harry Evans Back to the Newspaper Business.

5. SON OF ROSEMARY Ira Levin *(Dutton, $22.95)* God only knows what possessed Levin to birth this sequel to *Rosemary's Baby* (could it be...Satan?), but the result is most distressing—a kind of what-the-hey millennial cross between *The Kiss* and a certain infamous *Dallas* episode. Too bad the master of urbane horror (*The Stepford Wives, Deathtrap*) has finally sold his soul.

1. MEG Steve Alten *(Doubleday, $22.95)* Wistfully, one recalls the licentious preppies who rolled around in the sand—and were duly punished—in *Jaws*. Their '90s counterparts: grim, Crichton-esque lab coats, whom one is not sorry to see gobbled by the shark's fearsome ancestor, *Carcharodon megalodon*. A draining would-be *Jurassic Shark*.

2. HORNET'S NEST Patricia Cornwell *(Putnam, $25.95)* Give the crime queen credit for risking a novel sans the heroine who made her famous. Okay, now take it back. *Nest* could have used Dr. Kay Scarpetta—and a less clichéd setup (cub reporter paired with tough-talkin' deputy chief), fewer gross stereotypes

BEST SELLERS

GOOD NEWS, EGGHEADS: 1997 proved that literary fiction and filthy lucre are not mutually exclusive. On the contrary, Charles Frazier's *Cold Mountain* and Arundhati Roy's *The God of Small Things* alighted quietly on the charts and then refused to leave. Thomas Pynchon's *Mason & Dixon* was *the* beach read of the summer; Kurt Vonnegut's *Timequake* moved many; and Don DeLillo's gargantuan *Underworld* was presumably not *too* much for the nearly 300,000 readers who dared enter its pages. —*AJ*

HARDCOVER FICTION	WEEKS ON '97 LIST
1. THE NOTEBOOK *Warner*, Nicholas Sparks	44
2. THE PARTNER *Doubleday*, John Grisham	32
3. COLD MOUNTAIN *Atlantic Monthly*, Charles Frazier	26
4. PLUM ISLAND *Warner*, Nelson DeMille	20
5. THE GOD OF SMALL THINGS *Random House*, Arundhati Roy	20

HARDCOVER NONFICTION	WEEKS ON '97 LIST
1. SIMPLE ABUNDANCE *Warner*, Sarah Ban Breathnach	51
2. ANGELA'S ASHES *Scribner*, Frank McCourt	51
3. CONVERSATIONS WITH GOD, BOOK I, *Putnam*, Neale Donald Walsch	45
4. INTO THIN AIR *Villard*, Jon Krakauer	34
5. MEN ARE FROM MARS, WOMEN ARE FROM VENUS *HarperCollins*, John Gray	33

MASS-MARKET PAPERBACKS	WEEKS ON '97 LIST
1. DR. ATKINS' NEW DIET REVOLUTION *Avon*, Dr. Robert C. Atkins, M.D.	48
2. THE RUNAWAY JURY *Dell/Island*, John Grisham	30
3. ABSOLUTE POWER *Warner*, David Baldacci	18
4. THE LOST WORLD *Ballantine*, Michael Crichton	17

TRADE PAPERBACKS	WEEKS ON '97 LIST
1. CHICKEN SOUP FOR THE WOMAN'S SOUL *Health Communications*, J. Canfield, M.V. Hansen, J. Read Hawthorne, M. Shimoff	50
2. THE COLOR OF WATER *Riverhead*, James McBride	41
3. SHE'S COME UNDONE *Washington Square Press*, Wally Lamb	40
4. A CIVIL ACTION *Vintage*, Jonathan Harr	40
5. DON'T SWEAT THE SMALL STUFF... *Hyperion*, Richard Carlson	37
6. INTO THE WILD *Doubleday/Anchor*, Jon Krakauer	34

Source: *Publishers Weekly*; 1997 longest-running best-sellers

CELINE & JULIE GO

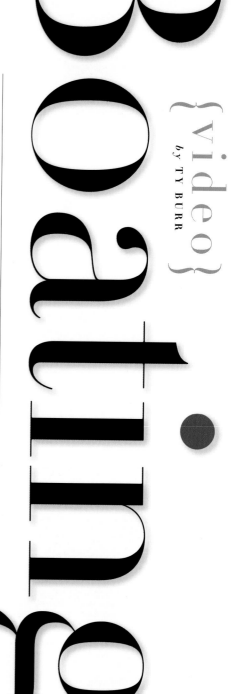

Boating

{video}

by TY BURR

1 *(New Yorker, unrated)* All right, it's a 23-year-old, 187-minute French film that makes *Seinfeld* look like it's about Something. But one of home video's continuing pleasures is the way it coughs up shimmering gifts from out-of-the-way corners of movie history. And there was no richer, sunnier, better video released in 1997 than Jacques Rivette's long-lost cult film about two women's journey down the rabbit hole of fantasy. Julie (Dominique Labourier, red-haired and decisive) and Céline (Juliet Berto, sloe-eyed and dreamy) meet in lazy, off-season Paris and circle around each other like playful alter egos. Gradually, they stumble into a mystery: a quiet suburban house where the same turgid melodrama plays out day after day, involving two frail sisters (Bulle Ogier and Marie-France Pisier), a hunky widower (*Reversal of Fortune* director Barbet Schroeder), and a doomed little girl. In short, this is a house of Fiction, and our two heroines determine to bust open the cloistered narrative and rescue the child. The plot unwinds so slowly as to exasperate metabolisms weaned on MTV shock cuts. Stay with it, though, and you'll discover a tale that reflects on the way we watch movies, and a comedy wise enough to recharge your soul.

Video of the YEAR

2 MESSAGE TO LOVE: THE ISLE OF WIGHT—THE MOVIE *(Sony Music, unrated)* If *Woodstock* is the hippie utopia of '60s concert films and *Gimme Shelter* the bad-acid nightmare, then this is the brain-dead reality. The 1970 Isle of Wight festival was a botch from the get-go: Some performers refused to play unless paid in cash, the stage caught fire, and a radical mob turned the event into an idiotic "people's festival." Yes, here's Jimi Hendrix scorching the strings 18 days before his death (plus the Doors, the Who, and Joni Mitchell). More to the point, here's emcee Rikki Farr whining "We put this festival on—you *bastards*—with a lot of love!" When your kids ask what the '60s were like, show 'em this—if you dare.

3 LONE STAR *(Columbia TriStar, R)* John Sayles' movies play like great, vivid novels—you can re-rent them the way you return to a favorite book. In this one, Chris Cooper plays a sad-faced Texas sheriff forced to face down the ghosts of his hero-cop father (Matthew McConaughey) and his father's rival (a snarling Kris Kristofferson). Hollywood would have turned this into a thunderous showdown, but Sayles knows *Lone Star*'s real battle—between dead parents and living children—can't be resolved with explosions. Instead, he gives us a town's teeming characters and caps the film with a love scene that would shock if it weren't so calm with forgiveness.

4 PARADISE LOST: THE CHILD MURDERS AT ROBIN HOOD HILLS *(Cabin Fever, unrated)* "To me, this place, as I stand, is like hell on earth." So says the stepfather of one of three boys killed in 1993 in West Memphis, Ark. But it could also have been said by the three teens convicted of the murders, whose only crime, this documentary suggests, was their penchant for black clothes, Metallica records, and Wicca. Long, grisly, and unfathomably sad, *Paradise* cracks the facade of small-town America and lets the demons loose.

5 FLY AWAY HOME *(Columbia TriStar, PG)* Remember *The Black Stallion*? Director Carroll Ballard and cinematographer Caleb Deschanel reunite for this shaggy-goose story of a girl mourning her mother's death (Anna Paquin), her inventor dad (Jeff Daniels), and the flock of geese that follow her everywhere, including into the sky when she teaches them how to migrate. It's fun, all right, but there's also a pained awareness of human and ecological mortality that makes the film beautifully uncondescending for older children and their parents.

6 STAIRWAY TO HEAVEN *(Columbia TriStar, PG)* WWII pilot David Niven was supposed to die—he jumped without a parachute, after all—but his angel missed him in the fog, and now Niven's fallen in love and won't go quietly. Another fever-dream classic from codirector Michael Powell (*The Red Shoes*), 1946's *Stairway* was finally given its video due this year with a print that restores its vibrant colors (for the earthly sequences) and crisp black-and-whites (for the heavenly scenes). It's clever, heartfelt, impeccably crafted—and just a little nuts.

7 JERRY MAGUIRE *(Columbia TriStar, R)* Yeah, it's old news, but it hit video stores in 1997, and it's still the most substantial and emotional comedy to come out of Hollywood in aeons. Does it finally prove that Tom Cruise is a great actor? Or does it merely provide him with the ultimate Tom Cruise role—deeper, funnier, and more accountable than ever? Doesn't matter: The real plaudits should go to writer-director Cameron Crowe, who shows us every stage in the humanization of Jerry the Jerk with grace, bemusement, and—most unheard of in Studioland—a willingness to listen to the characters.

8 MISS EVERS' BOYS *(HBO, PG)* This made-for-cable drama deals powerfully with a nasty chapter in U.S. history: the infamous Tuskegee study, in which black men with syphilis were denied treatment so their long-term symptoms could be noted. It's tightly directed, too, by veteran Joseph Sargent. But the reason to rent it is to watch one of the best actresses of our time—that would be Alfre Woodard—sink her teeth into the role of project nurse Eunice Evers, a woman standing, paralyzed, at the intersection of complicity and compassion.

9 GROSSE POINTE BLANK *(Hollywood, R)* The concept seems off-puttingly high—Hitman Goes to High School Reunion—but the execution, appropriately, is spot on. John Cusack is broodingly chatty as the class cipher who returns 10 years later with a business in, um, removals, and a wuzzy case of the hots for his once-and-future prom date (Minnie Driver, giving as good as she gets). The movie's not perfect—Dan Aykroyd keeps dragging it toward slapstick as a rival killer—but *Blank* knows, and nails, the primal fear that only a 10-year reunion can engender.

10 THE UMBRELLAS OF CHERBOURG *(LIVE, unrated)* A love story—about a shop girl (Catherine Deneuve, 20 years old and so innocent) and a mechanic (Nino Castelnuovo)—that's sung to the swoony music of Michel Legrand. Thirty-three years on, the late Jacques Demy's vision has aged with exquisite grace, and the new video release makes the never-never-land colors seem more hyperreal than ever. This is how young lovers see the world: privileged, melodic, and blissfully naive.

5 WORST

NO MAN IS AN ISLAND: But *Dr. Moreau*'s Brando comes pretty close

1. EVITA *(Hollywood, PG)* Madonna is just fine in what may be her most emblematic film role to date, but, face it, it's a dreadful movie, and on video it's even worse, like watching a hyperactive historical tableau through the wrong end of the binoculars. There's no plot, just an endless parade of marches, explosions, chowderheaded lyrics, and chilly star worship. Director Alan Parker's the fall guy here, coming off like Leni Riefenstahl drunk on Broadway sentiment.

2. HONEY, WE SHRUNK OURSELVES *(Walt Disney, PG)* Disney found profits cloning its animated franchises for the video market—*Aladdin* and *Beauty and the Beast* have both spawned straight-to-tape sequels—but the low-budget chintz really shows in this purposeless attempt to "extend" a live-action franchise. It's hard to tell what's shrinking faster here: narrative inspiration or Rick Moranis' career.

3. THE ISLAND OF DR. MOREAU *(New Line, PG-13)* How *bad* is this version of the H.G. Wells novel? Start with Marlon Brando wearing an ice bucket on his head for no reason. Move on to the blender-size homunculus who accompanies him. Don't miss Val Kilmer's Brando impression that wavers between genius and a party trick. In fact, don't miss this movie: Rent it with an Ed Wood film and watch the torch being passed.

4. ANY VIDEO FROM JERRY SPRINGER *(Real Entertainment)* Jerry Springer's *Too Hot for TV!* and *Jerry Springer's Wild Relationships!* play like outtakes from Mullet Nation: down-market guys and gals pummeling each other during tapings of "I'm So Dumb I Cheated on Myself" (okay, I made it up—but it wasn't hard). Alternately hilarious and depressing, this is the closest yet to anthropological porn.

5. VAMPIRELLA *(New Horizons, unrated)* Tinkertoy sets, Radio Shack special effects—yep, it's a Jim Wynorski movie. The auteur of *Sorority House Massacre 2* louses up the chance to make a good trashy/sexy flick out of the '70s comic about a fanged babe from Drakulon. Talisa Soto's bikini shows more emotion than her performance, and as the villain, Roger Daltrey torpedoes what's left of his career.

TOP VIDEOS

ALTHOUGH TOM CRUISE SPENT MOST OF LAST YEAR squirreled away on the secretive set of Stanley Kubrick's *Eyes Wide Shut*, his fans kept in touch by way of *Jerry Maguire*—1997's No. 1 rental. But then, *Maguire* had the advantage of a midyear release date. By another measure, *Men in Black* was the year's top tape: The video, which appeared in November, had the biggest debut of 1997, racking up a colossal 118 rentals per store in the first week it was available. —*Troy Patterson*

Rank	Title	Revenue
1. JERRY MAGUIRE *Columbia TriStar*, **Tom Cruise**		**$60.19**
2. LIAR LIAR *Universal*, **Jim Carrey**	57.41
3. A TIME TO KILL *Warner*, **Matthew McConaughey**	50.71
4. THE FIRST WIVES CLUB *Paramount*, **Bette Midler**	47.84
5. RANSOM *Touchstone*, **Mel Gibson**	46.78
6. PHENOMENON *Touchstone*, **John Travolta**	46.24
7. SCREAM *Dimension*, **Neve Campbell**	44.91
8. MICHAEL *Warner*, **John Travolta**	42.51
9. THE LONG KISS GOODNIGHT *New Line*, **Geena Davis**	41.35
10. SLEEPERS *Warner*, **Jason Patric**	41.02
11. THE GHOST AND THE DARKNESS *Paramount*, **Val Kilmer**	40.34
12. ABSOLUTE POWER *Warner*, **Clint Eastwood**	38.29
13. THE ROCK *Hollywood*, **Nicolas Cage**	37.59
14. KINGPIN *MGM/UA*, **Woody Harrelson**	37.54
15. MEN IN BLACK *Columbia TriStar*, **Will Smith**	37.46
16. THE DEVIL'S OWN *Columbia TriStar*, **Harrison Ford**	36.23
17. TIN CUP *Warner*, **Kevin Costner**	34.90
18. THE GLIMMERMAN *Warner*, **Steven Seagal**	34.05
19. JACK *Hollywood*, **Robin Williams**	33.54
20. JUNGLE2JUNGLE *Walt Disney*, **Tim Allen**	31.86
21. FACE/OFF *Paramount*, **Nicolas Cage**	31.77
22. THE SAINT *Paramount*, **Val Kilmer**	31.67
23. MURDER AT 1600 *Warner*, **Wesley Snipes**	30.79
24. THE FAN *Columbia TriStar*, **Robert De Niro**	30.64
25. THE LOST WORLD: JURASSIC PARK *Universal*, **Jeff Goldblum**	29.42

Note: Figures are 1997 rental revenues, in millions; source: VSDA VidTrac

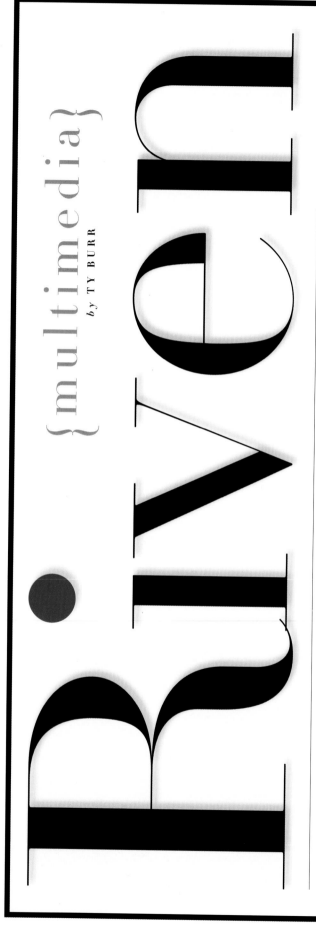

{multimedia}

Riven

by TY BURR

1 The interactive industry is obsessed with the latest, the fastest, the shiniest. So why are we choosing as 1997's best a CD-ROM sequel that hews so closely to its 1993 forebear? Sure, *Riven* represents a technological advance on the original *Myst*—still the best-selling computer game of all time—but what's most impressive is that it dares to stick with what worked the first time around. Only in this case, it's *more* serene, *more* otherworldly—a bigger, better space in which to lose yourself. ◆ Brothers Rand and Robyn Miller, along with production designer and Disney refugee Richard Vander Wende, may have built *Riven* with SGI workstations instead of the garage-bound Macs that hatched *Myst*, but the upgrade is noticeable mostly in the details—in the birds soaring in the distance and the natives scurrying into the woodwork. Even the fantasy-based narrative you slowly uncover in your rovings is a secondary pleasure. The most striking thing here is the generosity of the experience—the stubbly, old-world textures of the walls, the visual ingenuity of the puzzles, the leviathan secrets revealed by an underwater window. *Riven* is so richly imagined that it's very nearly a vacation, and it's soothing enough to qualify as therapy. Its grace shows up the multimedia industry's twitch-game mentality for the shallow adolescent posturing it is and points the way toward virtual realities to come.

2 VIRTUAL SPRINGFIELD
One reason *The Simpsons* is arguably the most brilliant show on TV is that every corner of every frame seems packed with a gag. Project that wisenheimer-smorgasbord feel onto a CD-ROM, and you have *Virtual Springfield*, the closest you'll get to poking into Mr. Burns' desk. Astounding in its variety of places to go, it's nirvana for *Simpsons* fetishists and just hilarious for everyone else.

3 MARS PATHFINDER LANDING
The way boomers recall clustering around the TV when Neil Armstrong moonwalked and Gen-Xers recall the *Challenger* explosion, today's kids may one day see the *Pathfinder* mission as their defining cultural event—and the Internet as the medium that gave it to them. You could catch the footage on CNN—but how much richer the experience was on the Web, via the NASA, CNN, and MSNBC sites or any of the smaller fan pages that provided scientific perspective and unscientific awe. It was as signal an event for cyberspace as for real space: the week the world turned to the Net for the real deal.

4 PALMPILOT
Remember the derision visited upon the Apple Newton, the first real personal digital assistant? Even Mike Doonesbury would have to change his tune now that 3Com's PDA has proved that a li'l pocket computer really can replace address books, schedulers, E-mailboxes, Gameboys, and more. The genius of the PalmPilot is that anyone can customize software for it, and it easily synchs up with your PC or Mac, making it a snap to load up all the information you need. The downside? The cultlike nature of its adherents: This may be the first PDA to inspire actual Public Displays of Affection.

5 PARAPPA THE RAPPER
Too many videogames are grim, goal-obsessed obstacle courses, but not this bonkers Sony PlayStation title. A huge hit in Japan, *Parappa* has the regurgitated neon giddiness that marks many of that country's pop pleasures: Imagine the Banana Splits making like the Fresh Prince in a karaoke bar. The aim is to help a floppy-eared cartoon doggie learn to rap and thus win over his flower girlfriend, but it's the whimsical visual design and cartoony rap songs that make this irresistible for parents and—oh, yeah—kids.

6 DRIVEWAYS OF THE RICH AND FAMOUS
(www.driveways.com) Why download bogus nude pictures of Julia Roberts when you can get a gander at her actual driveway? Pitched with such dryness that it's impossible to say whether it's a goof on celebrity

YO, MY TV RAPS! Parappa gets down

mania or the genuine article, John Cunningham's site (an outgrowth of his L.A.-based public-access cable show) lets you peer at the carports and entryways of stars from A (Steve Allen) to Z (Pia Zadora). Best are the deadpan interviews with gardeners, mailmen, and pizza-delivery guys.

7 GOLDENEYE 007
One of the few Nintendo 64 games to take advantage of the platform's cinematic sweep, this James Bond game sticks close to the basic plot outline of the Pierce Brosnan movie while tossing in fave Bondian bad guys from the past (Richard Kiel's Jaws, Grace Jones' May Day). In fact, with witty memos from stalwarts M, Q, and Moneypenny, this may satisfy 007 addicts more than the recent movies themselves. Slip into your tux, sip that martini—and duck.

8 UN-CABARET
(www.uncabaret.com) "WARNING: Some of these clips contain potentially *offensive language*. Others contain even more *disturbing ideas*. Welcome to planet Earth." After three years, this online extension of comic Beth Lapides' weekly alternative-yuks salon at L.A.'s Luna Park remains dicier and funnier than many other supposedly cutting-edge showcases. *Saturday Night Live*? Puh-leeze. Both Julia Sweeney and Colin Quinn are actually allowed to make you laugh here. The sound and video clips are swell, and the streaming audio in the "Cancer World" section bodes well for the future. But c'mon, Beth, when will you broadcast the show live?

9 MAPQUEST
(www.mapquest.com) Frighteningly handy, this is one site that can sell even a hardened Luddite on the medium's potential. Type in a street address anywhere in the U.S., Canada, or London, and up pops a map on your browser. Pull back for a view of the neighborhood, town, county, or entire country. Punch in two addresses and get driving directions and maps. Now figure out a way to install your PC in your car dashboard.

10 FRAY
(www.fray.com) As cyberspace grows more crowded with webzines that bristle with opinions and self-importance, this calm, compassionately disturbing site seems more and more an oasis of grace. Derek Powazek and his gang take brief personal anecdotes from readers and turn them into affecting online morality plays. The subjects are drugs, work, relationships, and crime, and the tone is that of a late-night confession. From a design standpoint, *Fray* is stunning, but it's the content—and the way it resonates with a reader's own life—that makes it stick.

1. DIGITAL PETS And, lo, the land was filled with the whining of children whose parents had forgotten to feed the Tamagotchi, the whimpering of dogs gone unwalked as pubescent owners obsessed over pixel pals, the sobbing of tots coming to grips with the mortality of a high-tech stopwatch. As a fad, it was right up there with Pet Rocks, but it was as a barometer of schoolyard self-absorption that the digipet craze was most depressing.

2. PUSH TECHNOLOGY For all the hype about Point-Cast, Microsoft's channel-definition format, and other devices that shove the latest news and weather down the pipe to your computer, push technology smells like information overload taken to its illogical conclusion. How many people do you know who have downloaded Point-Cast's software, watched their system slow to a crawl whenever it went into retrieval mode, disconnected—and turned on the TV?

3. MURDER MAKES THE MAGAZINE (www.amazon. com/exec/obidos/stores/excbdev) As a marketing stunt, this was sheer genius. More than 400,000 entrants took novelist John Updike up on his online offer to complete the tale of beleaguered magazine editrix Tasso Polk (44 contestants made the cut), and sponsor/cyberbookstore Amazon.com got the kind of publicity most websites dream of. But as literature—well, let's just note that too

5 WORST

many cybercooks spoil the gruel, and that the finished *Murder* is grueling indeed.

4. POSTAL Videogame violence is in the eye of the beholder, certainly—the carnage that horrifies parents is exactly what endears *Quake* to teenage boys—but this waste-'em-all shooter (recently banned in Australia) from Ripcord shreds the envelope with deeply clueless cynicism. Kids! Be the first on your block to make like a real live spree killer, mow down random passersby, and listen to them groan for mercy! If only this allowed you to go gunning for Tamagotchis…

5. DIGITAL GRIDLOCK AOL's ongoing brownouts and E-mail outages. The torpor that hits your Web browser in the late afternoon. That stressed-out server that won't pony up the page you want. With more and more people piling onto the Internet, and with high-cholesterol multimedia files coming into their own, the Information Superhighway is already in dire need of more lanes. Expect things to get much worse before they get better—and expect to eventually pay extra for premium (i.e., faster) service.

MAIL BOMB: *Postal* man always shoots twice

TOP CD-ROMS

ALTHOUGH THE JUSTICE DEPARTMENT made Microsoft squirm in '97, the software behemoth's *Windows 95 Upgrade* maintained its lock on the top spot of the best-selling CD-ROM chart for a second year. Meanwhile, the hotly anticipated *Myst* sequel, *Riven*, sold nearly half a million copies (landing at No. 6 on the chart), despite its late-October release. —*Kipp Cheng*

1. MICROSOFT WINDOWS 95 UPGRADE *Microsoft*		935,917

2. VIRUSSCAN *McAfee*	681,976	14. MONOPOLY GAME *Hasbro Interactive*	307,873
3. MYST *Brøderbund*	669,526	15. MICROSOFT GREETINGS WORKSHOP *Microsoft*	282,373
4. DIABLO *CUC Software*	603,823	16. MICROSOFT PUBLISHER *Microsoft*	280,413
5. MICROSOFT FLIGHT SIMULATOR *Microsoft*	592,393	17. TROPHY BASS *CUC Software*	267,219
6. RIVEN: THE SEQUEL TO MYST *Brøderbund*	473,287	18. PRINT SHOP ENSEMBLE III *Brøderbund*	265,371
7. TURBOTAX DELUXE *Intuit*	471,396	19. PRINTMASTER GOLD DELUXE PUBLISHING SUITE *Mindscape*	261,198
8. NORTON UTILITIES *Symantec*	396,440	20. PRINTMASTER GOLD PUBLISHING SUITE *Mindscape*	260,363
9. QUICKEN DELUXE *Intuit*	369,081	21. QUAKE *GT Interactive*	258,581
10. COMMAND & CONQUER: RED ALERT *Virgin*	340,701	22. FIRST AID DELUXE *Cybermedia*	258,136
11. MICROSOFT OFFICE PRO 97 *Microsoft*	338,820	23. BARBIE FASHION DESIGNER *Mattel*	255,520
12. PRINT SHOP DELUXE III *Brøderbund*	320,968	24. QUICKEN *Intuit*	252,978
13. NASCAR II *CUC Software*	318,217	25. X-WING VS. TIE FIGHTER *LucasArts*	249,121

Note: Chart covers period 1/97–11/97; source: PC Data

Bowing Out

WHENEVER ONE OF THE GREAT STARS OF HOLLYWOOD PASSES ON, IT'S THE FASHION to call him or her an "institution." That word belittles James Stewart, whose great gift was for seeming life-size. Think of all the other gods of the silver screen—stoic creatures, massive and glamorous—and then think of Stewart's lowered head, canny stammer, and bashful, democratic gaze. He's not sure about this movie stardom thing—it seems as if he'd rather be sitting with you in the fifth row of the Bijou, sharing popcorn and muttering, "Wouldja *look* at that?"

It was never an act, but there was far more craft to it than Stewart, who died July 2 at 89, usually got credit for. His most beloved roles are his most forthright: Jefferson Smith making honesty's last stand on the Senate floor in *Mr. Smith Goes to Washington*; Mike Connor caving in to Hepburn's luminosity in *The Philadelphia Story* (the role that won him a Best Actor Oscar); Elwood P. Dowd toasting his invisible rabbit companion in *Harvey*; above all, George Bailey rediscovering small-town verity in *It's a Wonderful Life*. Not to denigrate the films or his performance in them, but they console rather than rankle, and Stewart knew there was more to life—and acting—than that.

He didn't get much chance to explore during the '30s; MGM kept him too busy in fluff like *The Gorgeous Hussy* and classics like *The Shop Around the Corner*, and, besides, he was having too much fun playing the ladies' man with Marlene Dietrich, Ginger Rogers, and Olivia de Havilland. But when Stewart returned from World War II Europe, where he had risen to colonel and flown more than 20 bombing missions, he entered a period of disillusionment that was resolved only with his discovery of Westerns on the screen and Gloria Hatrick McLean off (they wed in 1949 and were together until her death in 1994). The five oaters he made with director Anthony Mann—1950's *Winchester '73* is the first, 1953's *The Naked Spur* is the best—revived the genre with a new and violent maturity, and Stewart was clearly thinking about the hard choices George Bailey's ancestors had had to face. With his pinnacles for Alfred Hitchcock, 1954's *Rear Window* and 1958's *Vertigo*, the actor probed the moral flaws behind his all-American veneer. The latter looks to be his single greatest performance: Obsessed with the two faces of Kim Novak, he gently leads us into voyeurism and necrophilia while never letting us lose sight of the sweet, simple, lost Jimmy of an earlier era.

In retrospect, however, *It's a Wonderful Life* remains his key movie, not because it ultimately makes us feel so good but because Stewart makes George Bailey's despair so harrowingly real. That he explicitly based that performance on his father—who ran an Indiana, Pa., hardware store into his 80s—tips Stewart's hand. He was a star because he stayed rooted in the ideals of small-town America. He was an artist because he knew the darkness that could hide there. —*Ty Burr*

ROBERT MITCHUM

BORN 1917

"THE BEAUTY OF THAT MAN," SAID ACTOR LEE MARVIN OF ROBERT MITCHUM. "HE'S SO STILL. HE'S MOVING AND YET HE'S NOT moving." In fact, there may have been no other performer during Hollywood's studio years who made contemptuous ease so integral to his appeal. Mitchum, who died July 1 at the age of 79, was one of the first movie stars whose persona commented on the absurdity of movie stardom itself; he was a postwar postmodernist whose blasé cool placed him above and beyond the neurotic machinations of the Hollywood factory. In 1948, he was arrested for possession of marijuana—a catastrophe that would have destroyed other careers—but the laconic, heavy-lidded mug that smirked out of news photos was more amused than apologetic. It's a measure of the times and of Mitchum that the bust made him a bigger star than ever.

To consider him lazy, however, is plain silly. Far from coasting on his rumpled charisma, Mitchum was one of the busiest actors in Hollywood—he made more than 130 films, all told—and his on-screen grace was the product of thoughtful, consistent exertion. He doesn't sweat in movies like the classic 1947 film noir *Out of the Past* or Nicholas Ray's moody 1952 *The Lusty Men* because that would betray the characters: men who've been too burned by the world to make sudden foolish moves, whose reserve is protective and, ultimately, flawed.

Mitchum's was the poise of the intelligent man with calluses on his hands: Before coming to movies, he worked on factory lines, on a freighter, as a nightclub bouncer—and spent a week on a Georgia chain gang for vagrancy. He also knew from evil, and when it came time to portray it, in his role as the homicidal preacher in Charles Laughton's incandescent 1955 *The Night of the Hunter*, Mitchum gave the performance of his career: Raging, soothing, torn between the love and hate tattooed on his fists, the actor painted a bogeyman far more subtle and scary than our modern movie slashers. Here was proof of exactly how much those deceptively sleepy eyes had seen. —*TB*

JAMES MICHENER

BORN 1907

THE MASTER OF THE HISTORICAL EPIC, JAMES MICHENER SPENT HALF A century galloping the globe, personally researching close to 40 books. Many were 1,000-pagers with sweeping names like *The Source*, *Poland*, *Centennial*, and *Space*—and altogether, they accounted for an astounding 75 million copies in print. But the author and philanthropist, who died of kidney failure at age 90 on Oct. 16, led a storied life himself: Orphaned as a baby and raised by a poor widow who may have been his biological mother after all, he won a scholarship to Swarthmore and wrote his first book, 1948's *Tales of the South Pacific*, while sitting in a Navy Quonset hut in World War II. Rodgers and Hammerstein turned *Tales* into a smash 1949 musical, Michener won the Pulitzer for his debut effort—and his career was launched. With *Hawaii*, his third book, he hit upon the formula that would make him one of the most successful novelists ever: carefully researched sagas, stuffed with hundreds of characters, that tell the story of a place from the beginning of time until yesterday. Michener was sometimes dismissed by critics for churning out pounds of edifying yarn, but he was unperturbed: "A storyteller," he figured, "is somebody who's going somewhere." And, oh, the places he went! —*Alexandra Jacobs*

BIGGIE SMALLS

BORN 1972

IN THE WORLD OF HIP-HOP, CHRISTOPHER WALLACE LOOMED LARGE—AND NOT ONLY BECAUSE HE PACKED 300 POUNDS ONTO HIS 6-FOOT-3 frame. From the beginning, Wallace presented himself as the genuine article: a rapper with an actual rap sheet acquired on the streets of Brooklyn. Rechristening himself the Notorious B.I.G., he was the real deal: Detailing ghetto life and death in that distinctive, thick-tongued way of his, he appeared to be one hip-hop act who wasn't playacting. Unfortunately, the real-world aspects of Wallace's life didn't end even there. On March 9, following in the footsteps of ill-fated rival Tupac Shakur, Wallace, 24, was gunned down in a still-unsolved drive-by shooting in Los Angeles. A few weeks later, his first posthumous album was released. Its title (*Life After Death*) and cover image (Biggie leaning on a hearse) made the connections between life and art even more horrific than Biggie himself might have imagined. —*David Browne*

MICHAEL HUTCHENCE

BORN 1960

BY HIS OWN RECKONING, INXS LEAD SINGER MICHAEL HUTCH-
ence was "bloody good at being a rock star."
And by the textbook definition of the term—
prodigious substance abuse, fancy sports cars,
and famous girlfriends, plus a side career in
film and occasional fisticuffs with paparazzi—
he was. But in the end, being a good rock star
wasn't enough for Hutchence, who apparently
hanged himself in his Sydney, Australia, hotel
room on Nov. 22. As he prepared for INXS' 20th-
anniversary tour, Hutchence, 37, was reportedly
depressed over the rancorous custody battle
between his fiancée, Paula Yates, and her ex-
husband, singer Bob Geldof. Hutchence may
have been pushed to the edge by the news that
Yates and the daughter he had with her, 16-
month-old Heavenly Hiraani Tiger Lily, wouldn't
be joining him in Australia for Christmas because of the ongoing custody battle. At the
funeral, a single tiger lily was among the flowers on his coffin. —*Matthew McCann Fenton*

BRANDON TARTIKOFF

BORN 1949

HE WASN'T CALLED "THE MOST SUCCESSFUL PROGRAMMER IN THE HISTORY OF NET-
work television" for nothing. Brandon Tartikoff, who died of Hodgkin's
disease on Aug. 27 at age 48, was television's original boy wonder,
signing on with NBC in 1977 and rising in three years to become, at
31, the youngest-ever president of NBC Entertainment. Talented and
competitive in equal measures, Tartikoff was largely credited with
turning the network in the early 1980s from an industry joke to a ratings powerhouse (its shows included *L.A. Law*, *Cheers*, and *The Cosby
Show*). After a near-fatal 1991 car crash, he moved his family to New
Orleans so his daughter could be treated for her accident injuries. A
programmer to the end, Tartikoff, who had formed his own TV production company in 1996, was working the phone in his Los Angeles
hospital room, pitching show ideas, just weeks before he died. —*MMF*

CHRIS FARLEY

BORN 1964

WHEN CHRIS FARLEY, THE LOVABLE LOUT WHO FOUND FAME ON *SATURDAY NIGHT LIVE* AND IN A STRING OF BOISTEROUS FRAT-BOY MOVIES, DIED ON DEC. 18 IN Chicago of a drug overdose at age 33, many were saddened—but almost no one was shocked. Several months earlier, Farley's manager, Marc Gurvitz, had admitted to worrying about Farley's taste for alcohol and drugs and had wondered out loud if he would die an untimely death, like another heavyset comic. "Will he go the route of John Candy if he's not careful? Of course he will."

Farley himself had told an interviewer in September, "Once I thought that if I just had enough in the bank, if I had enough fame, that it would be all right. But I'm a human being like everyone else. I'm not exempt." And Farley certainly found a lot of fame: From *SNL*, the obese comic and Second City veteran made a rare successful leap to feature films, starring in *Beverly Hills Ninja* and with pal David Spade in *Black Sheep* and *Tommy Boy*. But increasingly his erratic behavior, like his over-the-top hosting of the Oct. 25 *Saturday Night Live*, raised eyebrows in Hollywood and concerns among his many showbiz friends.

"I'm trying to grow up a little bit and be able to take off the red nose and floppy shoes when I need to," Farley said in another 1997 interview. "I want to be a husband soon and have a family. When you're wacky and crazy all the time, I don't think you can do both worlds. I'd like to have that other world." Sadly, he never did. —*MMF*

JOHN DENVER
BORN 1943

IN THE '70S, THE FORMER HENRY JOHN DEUTSCHENDORF JR. SANG OF MOUNTAIN RANGES, SUNSHINE, COUNTRY ROADS, AND COUNTRY BOYS. IT WAS CORNY, OLD-fashioned Americana, seemingly out of place in the Watergate years, but it worked: Denver's ebullient demeanor, clear-as-a-stream tenor, and homespun hits (including "Take Me Home, Country Roads," "Annie's Song," and "Sunshine on My Shoulders") made him a welcome respite as America headed into a post-'60s comedown. Soon Denver was ubiquitous on radio and TV, and even film (*Oh God!*), and he may have been the only performer under 50 who ever got to co-headline a TV special with Frank Sinatra. After his moment passed—a combination of changing public tastes, a drop in the quality of his songs and records, and the removal of his granny glasses, which left him with a harder, sterner look—Denver made news mostly during several drunk-driving arrests. His legacy, though, isn't simply the rugged opening chords to "Rocky Mountain High" but his devotion to environmental and political causes. (One of his greatest performances ever was his heartfelt anticensorship testimony at the 1985 congressional "porn rock" hearings.) The 53-year-old singer's plane crashed into Monterey Bay early last fall, for reasons that are still unknown; if the cause proves to be the weather, it may have been the only time nature failed him. —*DB*

CHARLES KURALT
BORN 1934

"I COME FROM WANDERING TRIBES," SAID CHARLES Kuralt. Indeed, the 62-year-old chronicler of the offbeat and endearing in American life, who died on the Fourth of July from lupus-related complications, had made a career of wandering. After eight years as a CBS correspondent in such far-flung places as Vietnam, the Congo, and Peru, Kuralt asked his bosses in 1967 to let him look inward to the American soul full-time, by driving around the country and doing stories on whatever caught his interest. They said yes, a bit reluctantly, and his legendary *On the Road* series was born. Kuralt—who went on to a 15-year stint hosting the folksy *CBS News Sunday Morning* and who, by the time he died, had won 13 Emmys—wrote his own epitaph years ago when he said, "I always wanted to know where the roads went." —*MMF*

THE HEART OF THE FASHION WORLD SKIPPED SEVERAL BEATS WHEN GIANNI VERSACE, 50, WAS SHOT TO DEATH OUTSIDE HIS MIAMI BEACH MANSION ON JULY 15. This son of a Calabria dressmaker grew up to be the proclaimed "king of frock and roll," a provocateur who fused craft, classicism, and pop culture into a single, vibrant whole—and, in the process, made fashion fun.

Versace borrowed promiscuously from any influence that caught his eye: Alexander Calder mobiles, Byzantine mosaics, motifs from the Greek and Roman ruins he played in as a child, or the style of dress from a local brothel he passed as a boy. More than a little of that sensibility was evident in the revealing black dress, held together with safety pins, that he designed for Elizabeth Hurley to wear to the London premiere of *Four Weddings and a Funeral*; it made headlines around the world. Competitors like Giorgio Armani accused Versace of reducing fashion to pornography. (He, in turn, accused Armani of being a bore.) But Versace never apologized for lacing his work with sexual suggestion: "Shorter! Tighter! Higher!" he would scream to tailors at his Milan studio. He was also a shrewd spin master whose shows, attended by famous friends and featuring rock music and dozens of models on stage at once, were more akin to cabaret acts than to fashion debuts. "We live in an era of contrasts," he said in 1990. "Everything is fast and mixed, like fast food and gourmet meals. I translate that into clothing."

Last July, Versace had retreated to his South Beach home to unwind after a show in Paris. Of his many homes around the world, he was reportedly fondest of this Spanish-style mansion on Ocean Drive. A man with little formal education in fashion (or anything else), Versace once reflected: "I want to be part of our time, our music, our books. I do not want to stabilize, but to represent our time." He did. —*MMF*

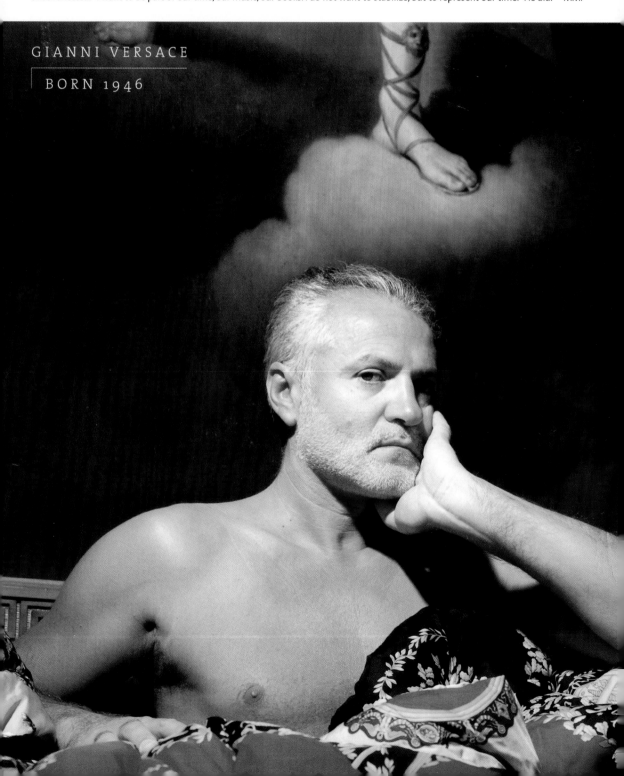

GIANNI VERSACE

BORN 1946

JEFF BUCKLEY
BORN 1966

THE MISSISSIPPI RIVER IS THE PRIME ARTERY OF AMERICAN POP. UNSTOPPABLE FORCES IN MUSIC have risen up along its banks, from the Delta bluesmen to Elvis Presley to the Replacements. This year, though, the Big River claimed someone who might have been destined to take his place in that elite group. When Jeff Buckley waded into a Memphis harbor and accidentally drowned May 29, the world lost more than a 30-year-old rocker with killer cheekbones. It lost a virtuoso guitarist, a songwriter whose soul-searching hymns suggested a budding Van Morrison or Joni Mitchell, and, most of all, a singer capable of angelic delicacy and demonic fire. It was Buckley's heart-stopping tenor that rose above the din of New York City folk clubs in the early '90s, when he landed a deal with Columbia Records. Like his father—folksinger Tim Buckley, who had died of a drug overdose in 1975 when he was only 28—Jeff Buckley sang like a hopeless romantic. Mysterious and brave, his music is best described by the 1994 title of his only full-length album: *Grace.* —*Jeff Gordinier*

FRED ZINNEMANN
BORN 1907

AN AUSTRIAN ÉMIGRÉ WITH ONLY A FEW ASSISTANT-CAMERAMAN JOBS TO HIS CREDIT, HE ARRIVED ALONE IN NEW YORK CITY IN 1929, ON THE SAME DAY THE STOCK market crashed. Zinnemann was undeterred. Indeed, throughout his distinguished directing career, one that included two Oscars for Best Director (for *From Here to Eternity* and *A Man for All Seasons*), Zinnemann, shown above with Audrey Hepburn, was known for his single-minded determination. He lavished attention to detail and showed an unusual ability to coax excellent performances from his actors in movies ranging from *High Noon* to *The Nun's Story* (he cast several stars in their first films—including Marlon Brando in 1950's *The Men* and Meryl Streep in 1977's *Julia*). Living in London in his last decades, Zinnemann remained interested in filmmak-ing—in late 1996 he protested plans to call an upcoming Bruce Willis film *The Day of the Jackal*, the title of his own 1973 classic thriller. "Let them call it *Night of the Shark* or something," he said. (The film was released last November, its title changed to *The Jackal*.) Zinnemann, 89, died in London on March 14, survived by his wife of 61 years. —*Nancy Bilyeau*

WILLIAM BURROUGHS

BORN 1914

IF "CREATIVITY COMES FROM A SERIES OF SHOCKS," AS WILLIAM S. BURROUGHS ONCE SAID, THEN THE BEATS' ELDER STATESMAN HAD CREATIVITY *DOWN*. THE PIS-tol-packing author, who was 83 when he died of a heart attack on Aug. 2, spent much of his career hooked on heroin. In 1951, he accidentally killed his common-law wife, Joan, while trying to shoot a whiskey glass off her head William Tell-style (he served 13 days in a Mexican jail). Most notable among his works was 1959's *Naked Lunch*, a collection of stream-of-consciousness dispatch-es from deep within his drug-addicted brain, and the source for some choice phrases in musical history ("heavy metal," "Steely Dan"). With his "cutup" technique of randomly juxtaposing texts, Burroughs acted as informal muse to the avant-garde, from rock-ers David Bowie and Patti Smith to filmmaker Gus Van Sant—in whose 1989 film *Drugstore Cowboy* he played an unrepentant junkie. And who could have predicted that this antiestablishment bad boy would appear in...a 1994 Nike ad? Shocking. —*AJ*

DAWN STEEL

BORN 1946

DAWN STEEL, THE SCRAPPY COLLEGE DROPOUT WHO GREW UP POOR IN AFFLUENT Great Neck, N.Y., made a small fortune marketing toilet paper imprinted with the Gucci logo, and went on to become the first woman ever to run a major studio, died Dec. 20 of a brain tumor at age 51.

She got her start in films planning the commercial tie-ins and licensing for the first *Star Trek* movie. Her shrewd campaign caught the attention of top Paramount execs, who put her in charge of all the studio's merchandising. Within seven years, Steel was in charge of movie production at the studio, overseeing a string of hits that included *Flashdance*, *Footloose*, *The Untouchables*, *Top Gun*, and *Fatal Attraction*.

In 1987, the same year that she gave birth to her only child, Rebecca, she moved over to become head of Columbia Pictures, the first woman to lead a major studio. Under her reign, the studio's films included such successes as *Awakenings*, *Ghostbusters 2*, and *Flatliners*. Yet when Steel left the studio to become an independent producer in 1991, she described her exit as an "escape...like I was let out of a cage." In a memoir she wrote in 1993, *They Can Kill You...But They Can't Eat You: Lessons From the Front*, Steel viewed her onetime membership in Hollywood's "boys' club" with some misgivings, aiming the book at women who, as she said, "want to be valued for cherishing their roles as mothers." Entertainment mogul David Geffen, a close friend, said that Steel had told him a few months before she died that "in retrospect, if she knew then when she was at the height of her career as a studio executive what she knew now, she would have had more children." —*MMF*

TOSHIRO MIFUNE

BORN 1920

TOSHIRO MIFUNE, 77, WAS OFTEN COMPARED TO JOHN WAYNE not only because of his many larger-than-life heroic performances in Japanese cinema but also for the body of work he produced with a single great director. Just as Wayne had John Ford, Mifune had Akira Kurosawa, and together the two made such masterpieces as 1950's *Rashomon* and 1954's *Seven Samurai*.

Shortly after World War II, Toho Studios was conducting a talent search when, according to Kurosawa's autobiography, an actress approached him, saying, "There's one who's really fantastic. But he's something of a roughneck. Won't you come have a look?" The would-be actor was an ex-soldier from the Japanese air force. For his audition, he reeled around the room "in a violent frenzy," then finished by flopping down in a chair to "glare menacingly." Says the director: "I am a person rarely impressed by actors. But in the case of Mifune I was completely overwhelmed."

While Mifune may be best known for such performances as the fierce thief in *Rashomon*, his films ran the gamut from heartrending tragedies to lighthearted romps—he played a swashbuckler general in *The Hidden Fortress*, a movie that was one of George Lucas' inspirations for *Star Wars*. Mifune also appeared in American productions like the TV miniseries *Shogun* (1980). Yet he made it clear which films meant the most to him. "I am proud of nothing I have done other than with him," he said of his partnership with Kurosawa. Mifune died on Dec. 24 in a hospital near his home in Tokyo. —*NB*

BURGESS MEREDITH

BORN 1909

REMEMBERED BEST FOR HIS HIGH-CAMP PERFORMANCES—THE PENGUIN ON TV'S *Batman* and the trainer Mickey in the *Rocky* films—Burgess Meredith was actually a classically trained actor viewed early in his career as an American Olivier. After being blacklisted in the 1950s for his leftist views, Meredith saw his career revive when Otto Preminger cast him in 1962's *Advise and Consent*—ironically, as an informer who wrecks careers with allegations of Communist influence. (He later won an Emmy for his portrayal of Joseph Welch, the lawyer who wrecked Joseph McCarthy, in the 1977 TV movie *Tail Gunner Joe*, a role he described as "a splendid revenge.") Meredith also earned Oscar nominations two years in a row for 1975's *The Day of the Locust* and 1976's *Rocky*. Still, it was his role as TV's Penguin, waddling about in top hat and monocle, that probably most resonates with baby boomers. "Of all the roles I've ever done," he said, "this is the first time my own kids have wanted to watch me." Indeed, in his 1994 memoir, Meredith, who died in Malibu on Sept. 9, recalled making his Broadway debut as a duck in 1932's *Alice in Wonderland* and added puckishly: "I went from a duck to a Penguin." —*MMF*

BRIAN KEITH

BORN 1921

FOR A GENERATION OF TELEVISION VIEWERS, BRIAN KEITH was everybody's favorite uncle. Known for playing swinging Manhattan bachelor "Uncle Bill" in the late-'60s sitcom *Family Affair*, Keith (shown with Sebastian Cabot, left) made the gruff, sturdy curmudgeon his stock-in-trade: He played similar roles (though this time out as the dad) in 1961's *The Parent Trap* and 1968's *With Six You Get Eggroll*—and again 15 years later as a hard-nosed crime-solving ex-judge in TV's *Hardcastle & McCormick*. Keith's diamond-in-the-rough character was no act: When the 75-year-old actor, apparently despondent over his advanced lung cancer and his 27-year-old daughter's suicide, died of a self-inflicted gunshot wound on June 24 in Malibu, *Family Affair* costar Johnnie Whitaker recalled: "He was a real Uncle Bill." —*MMF*

ALLEN GINSBERG
BORN 1926

THE LEGENDARY BEAT POET AND AUTHOR OF *HOWL* DIED APRIL 5 AT AGE 70 OF LIVER CANCER. WHEN TOLD JUST A WEEK EARLIER THAT HE WAS DYING, the longtime Buddhist accepted the news with stoic grace. In his final days he concentrated on capturing some thoughts in poetry and bidding farewell to an army of friends. To one of them, he said the day before slipping into a coma, "I'm dying, but I'm not worried—that's how it is." One of the last poems written by this merry prankster of American literature told friends, "I don't care what happens to my body/Throw ashes in the air." —*MMF*

NUSRAT FATEH
ALI KHAN

BORN 1948

QAWWALI MEANS "WISE UTTERANCE" IN ARABIC, AND THAT sums up perfectly the genius of Nusrat Fateh Ali Khan, who died of coronary arrest at age 48 in London. Khan did for *qawwali* what Bob Marley did for reggae, bringing the ecstatic, soaring vocals of the mystical Sufi sect of Islam to an international audience. In the process, he became Pakistan's most beloved musician and a world-music superstar, collaborating with such mainstream stars as Peter Gabriel and Eddie Vedder (on the soundtracks of *The Last Temptation of Christ* and *Dead Man Walking*, respectively). He died on Aug. 16, the 20th anniversary of the death of another popularizer of a once-obscure musical style, Elvis Presley. —*MMF*

LAURA NYRO

BORN 1948

IN 1966, A 17-YEAR-OLD FOLK PRODIGY NAMED LAURA NYRO impressed the then-white-hot Peter, Paul and Mary enough that they bought one of her songs on the spot for a $5,000 advance. "And When I Die" became a hit for the folk trio and set a pattern for Nyro's later success: Though she would never score in the top 20 herself, other artists would make gold records of Nyro's songs. The Fifth Dimension's cover of "Wedding Bell Blues" is best remembered, but there were others, for Barbra Streisand, Three Dog Night, and Blood, Sweat and Tears. A mosaic of influences, Nyro's music included folk, rock, classical, jazz, and blues. "When I write my music," the singer-songwriter once said, "I see all the rivers flowing—sensual, spiritual, religious, animal, intellectual." Nyro, who died on April 8 at age 49 of ovarian cancer, wrote in that first song bought by Peter, Paul and Mary: "I'm not scared of dyin' and I don't really care/If it's peace you find in dyin', well then let the time be near." —*MMF*

ALLAND, WILLIAM, 81
Producer, actor
(*Citizen Kane*); Nov. 11

ANDERSON, STIKKAN "STIG," 66
Manager of ABBA,
rock promoter; Sept. 12

ASHLEY, JOHN, 62
Actor, producer
(*The A-Team*); Oct. 3

AVERBACK, HY, 76
Actor, TV director-producer
(*M*A*S*H*); Oct. 14

AWDRY, WILBERT, 85
Author (*Thomas the Tank
Engine*); March 21

AXTON, MAE BOREN, 82
Singer, songwriter
("Heartbreak Hotel");
April 8

BAKER, LAVERN, 67
Legendary R&B belter;
March 10

BERRY, RICHARD, 61
Songwriter
("Louie, Louie"); Jan. 23

BEXLEY, DONALD, 87
Actor (*Sanford and Son*);
April 15

BING, SIR RUDOLF, 95
Metropolitan Opera
general manager; Sept. 2

BLACKSTONE JR., HARRY, 62
Magician and illusionist;
May 14

BLANE, SALLY, 87
Actress (*The Silver Streak*);
Aug. 27

BRAUN, MICHAEL, 60
Film and stage producer;
Jan. 27

BRUNER, WALLY, 66
TV personality and
ABC News correspondent;
Nov. 3

CAEN, HERB, 80
Pulitzer Prize-winning
newspaper columnist;
Feb. 1

CAIDIN, MARTIN, 69
Sci-fi novelist (*Cyborg*);
March 24

CASELOTTI, ADRIANA, 80
Actress, voice of Disney's
Snow White; Jan. 19

CHANDLER, DOROTHY, 96
Philanthropist and Oscar
pavilion namesake; July 6

CHEATHAM, "DOC," 91
Internationally known
jazz trumpeter; June 2

CLARKE, SHIRLEY, 77
Independent filmmaker
(*The Connection*); Sept. 23

CLASTER, NANCY, 82
Romper Room cocreator;
April 25

COMPTON, JOYCE, 90
Actress (more than
200 film credits); Oct. 13

CONNOLLY, BRIAN, 52
Glam-rocker (with
Sweet); Feb. 10

DAVIS, GAIL, 71
Actress (*Annie Oakley*);
March 15

DELFINO, FRANK J., 86
Actor (McDonald's
Hamburglar); Feb. 19

DICKERSON, NANCY, 70
CBS' first female TV
reporter; Oct. 18

DICKEY, JAMES, 73
Poet and novelist
(*Deliverance*); Jan. 19

DISNEY, LILLIAN, 98
Walt's widow, who gave
Mickey Mouse his first
name; Dec. 16

(3) DIXON, JEANE, 79
Washington, D.C.-based
astrologer; Jan. 25

(5) DOYLE, DAVID, 67
Actor (Bosley on
Charlie's Angels); Feb. 26

FENNEMAN, GEORGE, 77
TV announcer (*You Bet
Your Life*); May 29

FORE, EDITH, 81
TV commercial actress
("I've fallen and I can't
get up"); July 31

GOTELL, WALTER, 72
Actor (Alexis Gogol in
Bond films); May 5

GRAPPELLI, STÉPHANE, 89
Jazz violinist, composer;
Dec. 1

GUÉTARY, GEORGES, 82
Singer, actor (*An American
in Paris*); Sept. 13

GUILAROFF, SYDNEY, 89
Hollywood hairdresser
(for Marilyn Monroe and
others); May 28

HALLAHAN, CHARLES, 54
Actor (*Hunter*); Nov. 25

HEATHERTON, RAY, 88
Actor, singer;
father of Joey; Aug. 15

HEDGES, MICHAEL, 43
New Age/folk guitarist,
composer; Dec. 2

HICKEY, WILLIAM, 69
Actor (*Prizzi's Honor*),
drama teacher; June 29

HORNBERGER, H. RICHARD, 73
Author (*M*A*S*H*); Nov. 4

ITAMI, JUZO, 64
Japanese director
(*Tampopo*), actor; Dec. 20

JAECKEL, RICHARD, 70
Actor (*The Dirty Dozen*);
June 14

JAFFE, LEO, 88
Former Columbia Pictures
president; Aug. 20

JAMES, DENNIS, 79
TV emcee (*The New Price
Is Right*); June 3

JARRICO, PAUL, 82
Blacklisted screenwriter
and producer
(*Salt of the Earth*); Oct. 28

JONES, J. DAVID, 61
Aerial stunt coordinator
(*Apocalypse Now*); July 14

(8) KAYE, STUBBY, 79
Comic, actor; Dec. 14

KENNEDY, ADAM, 75
TV actor (*Gunsmoke*) and
novelist; Oct. 16

KINGSLEY, DOROTHY, 87
Screenwriter (*Pal Joey*);
Sept. 26

KOMACK, JAMES, 72
TV writer-producer
(*Welcome Back, Kotter*);
Dec. 24

KUTI, FELA ANIKULAPO, 58
Nigerian Afrobeat
superstar; Aug. 2

LAMPELL, MILLARD, 78
Screenwriter, TV writer
(*Rich Man, Poor Man*);
Oct. 3

LANE, BURTON, 84
Composer (*Finian's
Rainbow*); Jan. 5

LANE, RONNIE, 51
Rock bassist; cofounder of
Small Faces; June 4

5

6

7

8

COVERS

Basinger: photograph by Andrew Southam/CPI; Damon: Andrew Eccles/Outline; DeGeneres: Firooz Zahedi/Botaish Group; Diana: Patrick Demarchelier/Retna Ltd.; DiCaprio: Firooz Zahedi/Botaish Group; Dylan: Len Irish; Ford: photograph by Nigel Parry; agency: CPI; styling: Kim Debus/Jam Arts; hair: Michael Kriston; makeup: Michael Laudati; prop styling: Leah Levin; shirt: Boss Hugo Boss; chair: Wyeth, N.Y.; Hanson: photograph by Frank W. Ockenfels 3; Jewel: Outline; Weaver: photograph by Ruven Afanador; styling: Kym Cantor/Art Department; hair: Maury Hopson; makeup: Brigitte Reiss-Andersen; prop styling: Joelyne Beaudoin/JGK; Rock: Chris Buck/Outline; Spice Girls: Harry Borden/Katz/Outline; Stewart: hardcover: Ted Allan/MPTV; softcover: Everett Collection

ENTERTAINERS OF THE YEAR

9: Firooz Zahedi/Botaish Group; 12–13: Harry Borden/Katz/Outline; 17: (top) Len Irish; Mark Seliger; 19: styling: June Ambrose; prop styling: Bradley Garlock/Judy Casey, Inc.; hair: Mike Daddy/Carie Hart; makeup: Barry M. White/Zoli; clothes and belt: Thierry Mugler; 20: styling: Kym Cantor/Art Department; hair: Maury Hopson; makeup: Brigitte Reiss-Andersen; prop styling: Jocelyne Beaudoin/JGK; manicurist: Elissa Ferri/Fasia; tuxedo gown: Christian Dior; cane: Early Halloween; 23: styling: Heidi Tortorici/Cloutier; prop styling: Nic Tortorici/Cloutier; grooming: Bernadette Beauvais/Visages Style; clothing: leather coat: Giorgio Armani, Beverly Hills; 24: Mario Testino; 25: agency: Montage; styling: Denise Solis/Celestine; grooming: Catherine Furniss/Celestine; 26: Andrew Eccles; 27: agency: CPI; styling: Kim Debus/Jam Arts; prop styling: Leah Levin; hair: Michael Kriston; makeup: Michael Laudati; suit: Jil Sander; 28: styling: Mariska Nicholson/Celestine; hair: Helen Jeffers/Cloutier; makeup: Garen Tolkin/Cloutier; Edwards' shirt: Todd Oldham; skirt: XING by Jade at American Rag Cie; Eckhart's clothing: American Rag Cie; 29: agency: Edge; styling: Jennie Lopez/Edge; grooming: Akira/Garren NY; clothes: Giorgio Armani; 30: (top) Barron Claiborn; 32: (bottom) Swapan Parekh/PEOPLE; 34: agency: Botaish Group; styling: Alexander Gutierrez/Heller Artist; hair: Johnny Villanueva/Visages Style L.A.; makeup: Gucci Westman for Visages/Shu Uemura; dress: Fernando Sanchez; shoes: Missoni; 35: (bottom) Gwendolen Cates; 36: grooming: Catherine Furniss/Celestine; styling: Rita Rago; 37: Outline; 39: Librado Romero/*The New York Times*; 40: Greg Lavy/Outline; 41, 43: Brigitte Lacombe; 45: Len Irish/Outline; 47: Robert Maxwell

1997 BIG MOMENTS

48–49: Rex USA; 50: Dennis Kleiman/Retna Ltd.; 52: Susan Sterner/AP/Wide World Photos; 53: Steve Starr/SABA; 54: (left) USPS; AP/Wide World Photos; 56: Najlah Feanny/SABA; 58: James M. Kelly/Globe Photos; 59: Susan Sterner/AP/Wide World Photos; 60: Timothy White/Outline

BEHIND THE SCENES

62–63: Melinda Sue Gordon; 68: Ken Regan/Camera 5; 69: David James; 74–75: Merri Cyr; 77: Mark Tillie; 78–79: Ian Cook/PEOPLE

STYLE

80: (left) Frank Trapper/Sygma; Marissa Roth/Retna Ltd.; 81: (clockwise from top left) Marissa Roth/Retna Ltd.; Lisa Rose/Globe Photos (2); Marissa Roth/Retna Ltd.; 82: (Leeves, Hunt, Anderson, Baranski) Craig Skinner/Celebrity Photo; (Downey) Janet Gough/Celebrity Photo; 83: (clockwise from top left) Theodore Wood/Camera Press/Retna Ltd.; Kelly Jordan/Galella Ltd; Arnal/Geral/Charriau/Catarina/STILLS/Retna Ltd.; photograph by Kevin Mazur; Fitzroy Barrett/Globe Photos; Kevin Mazur; 84: (clockwise from top left) Steve Sands/Outline; Thomas Lau/Outline (2); Steve Azzara/Sygma; Photograph by Richard Mitchell; 85: (clockwise from top left) Steve Sands/Outline; Gerardo Somoza/Outline (3); 86: (clockwise from top) Marissa Roth; Jason Varney/Galella Ltd.; Steve Sands/Outline; 87: Steve Granitz/Retna Ltd.; Bill Davila/Retna Ltd.; Fitzroy Barrett/Globe Photos; Evan Agostini/Gamma-Liaison; 88: (clockwise from top left) Aslan/Barthelemy/Niviere/Roussier/Sipa Press; Lisa Rose/Globe Photos; Andrea Renault/Globe Photos; Kevin Winter/Celebrity Photo; Nina Prommer/Globe Photos; 89: Andrea Renault/Globe Photos; Fitzroy Barrett/Globe Photos; Chris Moody/Hutchins Photo; Andrea Renault/Globe Photos; Fitzroy Barrett/Globe Photos; Jim Smeal/Galella Ltd.

BEST & WORST

94: (top) J. Eisen; Merie W. Wallace; 95: Mark Tillie; 96: (top) Brian Hamill; Michel Del Sol; 97: (from top) Steven Vaughn; © Walt Disney; Tony Friedkin; Chuck Hodes; Sam Emerson; Robert Zuckerman; 98: John Bramley; 102: (top) Jack Roland; Stephen Danelian; 103: Eric Liebowitz; 104: Michael Ginsburg; 105: Alice S. Hall; 108: Dan Chavkin/Outline; 110: Kevin Mazur; 111: Michael Lavine/Outline; 115: Nigel Parry/CPI; 119: Peter Sorel; 122: Rodney A. Greenblat/Interlink; 123: Running With Scissors

BOWING OUT

125: Ted Allan/MPTV; 126: Ruven Afanador/Outline; 127: MOMA/Film Stills Archive; 128: Geoffrey De Boismenu/Outline; 129: (top) Chris Cuffaro/Outline; Gunther/MPTV; 130: Chris Buck/Outline; 131: (top) Jim McHugh/Outline; CBS/Archive Photos; 132: Helmut Newton/Sygma; 133: (top) Merri Cyr; Sanford Roth/AMPAS/MPTV; 134: Anton Corbijn; 135: (top) Darryl Estrine/Outline; Photofest; 136: (top) MOMA/Film Stills Archive; H. Gris/FPG; 137: Fred W. McDarrah; 138: Gabi Rona/MPTV; 139: (top) Cori Wells Braun/Outline; David Gahr; 140: (from top) Everett Collection; Timothy Greenfield-Sanders/Outline; Harry J. Siskind/Outline; 141: (from top) Photofest; Everett Collection; Archive Photos; Everett Collection; this page: Photofest